OPERA

TEXT:
ALESSANDRO TAVERNA

ILLUSTRATIONS BY:
ANDREA RICCIARDI, CLAUDIA SARACENI, SERGIO, THOMAS TROJER

BARRON'S

DoGi

English translation
© Copyright 1999
by Barron's Educational
Series, Inc.
Original edition © 1998 by
DoGi spa Florence, Italy
Title of original edition:
L'opera lirica
Italian edition by:
Alessandro Taverna
Consultant:
Stefano Catucci
Illustrations by:
Andrea Ricciardi
Claudia Saraceni
Sergio
Thomas Trojer
Graphic Display:
Francesco Lo Bello
Art Director:
Sebastiano Ranchetti
Page make up:
Sebastiano Ranchetti
Katherine Carson Forden
Iconographic researcher:
Katherine Carson Forden
Editorial Staff:
Andrea Bachini

English translation by:
Marion Lignana Rosenberg

HOW TO READ THIS BOOK

Each two-page spread is devoted to a major chapter in the history of opera, its places, and its leading figures. Several more technical pages cover the elements that make up an opera and the process by which an opera is born and takes form. The text on the upper left (1) and the large central illustration are devoted to the main subject. The columns in the margins (2) elaborate on the main theme or introduce its historical context. The other elements on the page—photos, reproductions of vintage prints, portraits—round out the presentation of the subject.

ACKNOWLEDGMENTS

ABBREVIATIONS:
t, top; *b,* bottom; *m,* middle; *r,* right; *l,* left.
ILLUSTRATIONS:
The illustrations contained in this volume, original and previously unpublished, were created at the request and under the supervision of DoGi spa, the copyright holder.

CREDITS:
Fausto Bianchi: 30–31; Stefano Bracelli: 24–25; Lorenzo Cecchi: 38–39, 56–57; Matteo Chesi: 14–15, 46–47; Mario Cossu: 26–27; Cesare D'Antonio: 6–7, 40–41; Tommaso Gomez: 22–23; L.R. Galante: 34–35; Andrea Ricciardi: 10–11, 32–33, 44–45; Claudia Saraceni: 28–29, 48–49, 52–53; Sergio: 4–5, 8–9, 20–21, 36–37; Giacomo Soriani: 12–13, 16–17, 42–43; Thomas Trojer: 18–19, 50–51, 54–55.
FRONTISPIECE: Andrea Ricciardi
COVER: Matteo Chesi
LIST OF REPRODUCTIONS:
DoGi spa made every effort to determine the possible rights of third parties and apologizes for any possible omissions or errors. They will gladly make necessary corrections in subsequent editions of this book.
(Works reproduced in their entirety are followed by the letter d; those from which a detail has been selected are followed by the letter d.)
6l Frontispiece for *Le Musiche di Jacopo Peri nobil fiorentino Sopra L'Euridice del sig. Ottavio Rinuccini, Rappresentato nello sposalizio della cristianissima Maria Medici Regina di Francia e di Navarra* (BIBLIOTECA MORENIANA, FLORENCE) e; **6r** Cesare Lisi, Interpretive Model of the Teatro Mediceo degli Uffizi, for the 1589 production, reconstruction (ARCHIVIO DELLA PROVINCIA, FLORENCE) e; **7** Bernardo Buontalenti, costume sketches for the *Intermezzi della Pellegrina,* 1589 (BIBLIOTECA NAZIONALE, FLORENCE) e; **8** Anonymous, *Presumed Portrait of Claudio Monteverdi,* seventeenth-century painting (RCS-IGDA, MILAN) d; **9l** Scene from the opera *L'Incoronazione di Poppea* by Claudio Monteverdi (TEATRO COMUNALE, BOLOGNA/PRIMO GNANI, MAGIC VISION, BOLOGNA) e; **9r** Design for Giovanni Legrenzi's opera *Germanico sul Reno,* for the 1675 production in Venice (RCS-IGDA, MILAN); **10** Anonymous, *Jean-Baptiste Lully,* seventeenth-century engraving (MUSÉE DU

CHATEAU, VERSAILLES) d; **11r** Felice Casorati, set design for *Dido and Aeneas* by Henry Purcell, Act I, Scene I, Maggio Musicale Fiorentino, 1940, tempera on wood, 21⁴/₅ × 27³/₄ in (55.5 × 70.5 cm) (TEATRO COMUNALE, FLORENCE) e; **11r** Anonymous, *Henry Purcell* (IGDA, MILAN) e; **14l** Thomas Hudson, *Georg Friedrich Händel,* painting (STAATSBIBLIOTHEK, HAMBURG) d; **15l** Anonymous, *The Celebrated Senesino's Landing in England* (IGDA, MILAN) e; **15r** Corrado Giaquinto, *Carlo Broschi, known as Farinelli* (CIVICO MUSEO BIBLIOGRAFICO MUSICALE, BOLOGNA) d; **16** Anonymous, *Pietro Metastasio,* engraving (IGDA, MILAN) e; **17l** A.M. Zanetti, *Caricature of the prima donna Francesca Cuzzoni and the castrato Nicolini* (FONDAZIONE GIORGIO CINI, ISTITUTO DI STORIA DELL'ARTE, VENICE) d; **17r** Anonymous, *Giovanni Battista Pergolesi,* painting (PINACOTECA CIVICA JESI) d; **19** Francesco Saverio Candido, *Domenico Cimarosa at the harpsichord,* 1785, oil on canvas, 50 × 40.15 in (127 × 102 cm) (MUSEO DI SAN MARTINO, NAPLES) d; **20** Joseph Siffred Duplessis, *Christoph Willibald Gluck at the spinet,* 1775, oil on canvas (KUNSTHISTORISCHES MUSEUM, VIENNA) d; **21l** Set design for *Iphigénie en Tauride* by Christoph Willibald Gluck, Maggio Musicale Fiorentino, 1981 (TEATRO COMUNALE, FLORENCE) e; **21r** Set design for *Dardanus* by Rameau, 1739 (BIBLIOTHEQUE DE L'OPÉRA, PARIS) e; **22** Franz Wolf, Costume for Papageno in *Die Zauberflöte* by Mozart, 1794–95, engraving (RHEINISCHE MUSEN) d; **22r** Anonymous, *Don Giovanni and Zerlina,* c. 1825, colored engraving (OSTERREICHISCHES THEATER MUSEUM, VIENNA, FOTO VOUK) d; **24** H. Mailly, *Caricature of Rossini on the occasion of his 75th birthday,* 1867 (GIANCARLO COSTA, MILAN) d; **25** Frontispiece of *Guillaume Tell,* lithograph (BIBLIOTHEQUE DES ARTS DECORATIFS, PARIS) d; **27l** C. Ferrario, Set design for *Norma,* print, 1898–99 (THÉÂTRE ROYAL ITALIEN, PARIS) e; **27r** Giuseppe Cammarano, *Vincenzo Bellini,* painting (IGDA, MILAN) e; **28** Girolamo Induno, *Gaetano Donizetti,* painting (IGDA, MILAN) e; **29** Early design for Max's costume in *Der Freischütz* (AKG, BERLIN) e; **30t** Pierre-Auguste Renoir, *The Theatre-Box,* 1874, 31¹/₂ × 25 in (80 × 64 cm) (COURTAULD INSTITUTE, LONDON) e; **30b** Anonymous, *Lorenzo Da Ponte,* engraving (FOTOTECA STORICA NAZIONALE)

e; **31** Anonymous, *Hugo von Hofmannsthal,* painting (IGDA, MILAN) e; **32** *Le Grand-Opéra de Paris* (ARCHIVES PHOTO FRANCE, PARIS) e; **33** Costume for the carnevale season for Gilbert Duprez in *Benvenuto Cellini* (MUSÉE DU LOUVRE, PARIS) e; **34** *Giuseppe Verdi* (SERGIO ANELLI, ELECTA) e; **35l** *Giuseppe Verdi and Arrigo Boito at Sant'Agata,* c. 1890 (MUSEO TEATRALE ALLA SCALA, MILAN) e; **35r** Gianni Vagnetti, Set design for *La Traviata* by Giuseppe Verdi, Maggio Musicale Fiorentino 1940, tempera and pencil on paper, 23 × 27¹/₂ in (58.5 × 70 cm) (TEATRO COMUNALE, FLORENCE) d; **36** *Richard Wagner,* 1868 (HULTON DEUTSCH COLLECTION) e; **37tl** *Bayreuther Festspiele* (BAYREUTNER FESTSPIELE, BAYREUTH/PHOTO JORG SCHULZE) e; **37tr** *Siegfried fights the dragon,* painting (RICHARD WAGNER MUSEUM, BAYREUTH) e; **37b** Scene for the production of *Parsifal* at the Bayreutner Festspiele, 1951 (BAYREUTNER FESTSPIELE, BAYREUTH) e; **39l** Edgar Degas, *Opera orchestra,* 1868–69, oil on canvas, 21 × 17³/₄ in (53 × 45 cm) (MUSÉE D'ORSAY, PARIS) e; **39r** *Gustav Mahler,* c. 1905 (HULTON DEUTSCH/BETTMANN) d; **40** Ilia Iefimovic Repin, *Modest Mussorgsky,* painting (NOVOSTI PRESS AGENCY, LONDON) e; **41l** Scene from *Eugene Onegin* in the 1973 Bolshoi Theatre production given at the Teatro alla Scala, Milan (TEATRO ALLA SCALA, MILAN) e; **41r** Piotr Konchalovsky, *Sergei Prokofiev,* 1934, painting (NOVOSTI PRESS AGENCY, LONDON) e; **42** *Giacomo Puccini* (RCS-IGDA, MILAN) e; **42b** Adolfo Hohenstein, Frontispiece for *Tosca* (VERDI-TOSCANINI CENTER, PARMA) e; **43** Scene from the production of *Cavalleria Rusticana* at the Teatro Comunale of Bologna (TEATRO COMUNALE, BOLOGNA/FOTO PRIMO GNANI, MAGIC VISION, BOLOGNA) e; **45** Prosper Mérimée, Set design for *Carmen* by Georges Bizet, 1846, watercolor (FOTO ARCHIVI FABBRI, MILAN) e; **45l** Soprano Mary Garden and tenor Jean Perrier in costume for *Mélisande and Pélléas* (BIBLIOTHEQUE DES ARTS DECORATIFS, PARIS) e; **45r** Léon Bakst, *Costume designs for Narcissus,* 1911, pencil, gouache, metallic paint on paper (THE FINE ART SOCIETY, LONDON) e; **46,** Egon Schiele, *Arnold Schönberg* (FISCHER FINE ART, LONDON) e; **47l** A scene from *West Side Story* (FOTO ARCHIVIO CURCIO EDITORE) e; **47r** Ferdinand Schmutzer, *Richard Strauss,* c. 1924, engraving (PROF. RUDOLF HARTMANN, MUNICH) e;

51l Giorgio de Chirico, Set design for *I puritani,* Act II, Scene I, Maggio Musicale Fiorentino 1933, tempera and pencil on paper, 14 × 17 in (35.5 × 43 cm) (TEATRO COMUNALE, FLORENCE) e; **51r** Bernardo Buontalenti, Designs for the first intermezzo, *Necessità con le tre parche,* 1589 (BIBLIOTECA NAZIONALE, FLORENCE) e; **51b** Oscar Kokoschka, Set design for *Un ballo in maschera,* Act I, Scene I, Maggio Musicale Fiorentino, 1963, lithograph, 29¹/₂ × 20¹/₂ in (75 × 52 cm) (TEATRO COMUNALE, FLORENCE) e; **53** Umberto Brunelleschi, Costume design for Turandot for Puccini's *Turandot,* Maggio Musicale Fiorentino 1940, tempera, pencil, and purpurin on paper, 14 × 10 in (36 × 26 cm) (TEATRO COMUNALE, FLORENCE) e; **52** Giacomo Manzù, Costume for Tristan for *Tristan und Isolde,* Teatro La Fenice, Venice, 1970–71 (DONAZIONE TIRELLI, MUSEO DEL COSTUME DI PALAZZO PITTI, FLORENCE) e; **54t** Max Reinhardt (IGDA, MILAN) d; **54b** Luca Roncomi (IGDA, MILAN) d; **55t** Luchino Visconti on the set of *The Twilight of the Gods* (MARSILIO EDITORE, VENICE); **57** *Philip Glass* (Linda Stone) d; **56b** Renzo Piano, *Section of the musical space installed in the Chiesa di San Lorenzo, Venice* (COLLEZIONE RENZO PIANO, GENOA) d; **58l** Chardin, Jean-Baptiste Siméon, *Jean-Philippe Rameau,* oil painting (LOUVRE, PARIS) d; **58r** Ludwig Schnorr and his wife Malvine in Wagner's *Tristan* (IGDA-DAGLI ORTI, MILAN) d; **59r** Illustration from the first edition of the opera *Orfeo ed Euridice,* published in Paris in 1764 (IGDA-DAGLI ORTI, MILAN) e; **60t** *The Bolshoi Theater of Moscow* (RCS, MILAN) e; **60b** *The Metropolitan Opera House of New York* in 1889 (RCS, MILAN) e; **61l** *Maria Callas* (IGDA-DAGLI ORTI, MILAN) e; **61r** *Luciano Pavarotti* (TEATRO ALLA SCALA, MILAN) e; **62l** *Claudio Abbado* (CURCIO, MILAN) e; **62r** *Herbert von Karajan* (RCS-IGDA, MILAN) e; **63** *Seiji Ozawa* (IGDA-DAGLI ORTI, MILAN) e.

COVER (clockwise from top left):
1. 45l; 2. 25; 3. 51r d; 4. 62l; 5. 24; 6. 39r; 7. 53; 8. 44; 9. 40; 10. 20; 11. 47l; 12. 28; 13. 29; 14. 51b; 15. 41r; 16. 39l d; 17. 51b; 18. Benjamin Britten (Erich Auerbach, 1973); 19. 42b; Cover illustration by Matteo Chesi.

BACK COVER: 42

CONTENTS

THE GREATS

The history of sung theater began in Florence more than 400 years ago, when groups of intellectuals sought to recreate the tragedies of ancient Greece. Musical drama or *melodramma,* born in noble courts, soon became popular with a wide public and spread throughout Europe in two forms, *opera seria* (tragic or serious opera) and *opera buffa* (comic opera), which led to the construction of specialized theaters. The greats of this extraordinary chapter in the history of art and of social custom were not only the composers, but also the authors of the texts set to music, the singers, the set designers, the impresarios, and (most recently) the conductors and stage directors.

♦ **PIONEERS**
Claudio Monteverdi (1567–1643), Jean-Baptiste Lully (1632–1687), Henry Purcell (1659–1695).

♦ **THE GENIUS OF THE 1700S**
Wolfgang Amadeus Mozart (1756–1791).

♦ **THREE LIBRETTISTS**
Pietro Metastasio (1698–1782), Lorenzo Da Ponte (1749–1838), Hugo von Hofmannsthal (1874–1929).

♦ **THE CLASSICAL AND ROMANTIC ERAS**
Gioacchino Rossini (1792–1868), Vincenzo Bellini (1801–1835),

Carl Maria von Weber (1786–1826), Giacomo Meyerbeer (1791–1864).

♦ **COMPOSERS OF THE 1700S**
Georg Frederick Händel (1685–1759), Domenico Cimarosa (1749–1801), Christoph Wilhelm Gluck (1714–1787).

♦ **THE GIANTS OF THE 1800S**
Giuseppe Verdi (1813–1901), Richard Wagner (1813–1883).

♦ **COMPOSERS OF THE 1800S**
Modest Mussorgsky (1839–1881), Peter Ilyich

Tchaikovsky (1840–1893), Hector Berlioz (1803–1869), Georges Bizet (1838–1875).

◆ **THE GREAT CONDUCTORS**
Arturo Toscanini (1867–1957), Herbert von Karajan (1908–1989), Leonard Bernstein (1918–1990).

◆ **THREE DIRECTORS**
Max Reinhardt (1873–1943), Luchino Visconti (1906–1976), Peter Sellars (1957–).

◆ **IMPRESARIOS** Louis Vernon, head Domenico Barbaja of the Paris Opera (1778–1841); (1798–1867).

◆ **TWO SET DESIGNERS**
Adolphe Appia (1862–1928), Nicola Benois (1901–1988).

◆ **GREAT SINGERS**
Carlo Broschi, known as Farinelli (1705–1782); Gilbert-Louis Duprez (1806–1896); Enrico Caruso (1873–1921).

◆ **THE 1900S**
Giacomo Puccini (1858–1924), Claude Debussy (1862–1918), Richard Strauss (1864–1949), Alban Berg (1885–1935), Benjamin Britten (1913–1976), Arnold Schoenberg (1874–1951).

◆ **BEL CANTO DIVAS**
Isabella Colbran (1785–1845), Giuditta Pasta (1797–1865), Maria Callas (1923–1977).

ORIGINS

The history of opera began in Florence. It was there, at the end of the sixteenth century, that a group of intellectuals who met at the home of Count Giovanni Bardi first thought of "renewing" the music of their times, inspired (as was often the case in the Renaissance) by classical culture and by Greek tragedy, in particular, its interweaving of words and music. This group called itself the Fiorentina Camerata; some of its members were mathematicians or poets, and all were musicians and singers. The members of the Camerata strove to create music that would accompany perfectly declaimed words, according to their idea of ancient Greek drama. The Medici court gave them the opportunity to experiment with this new type of performance. In its earliest days, opera was intimately tied to courtly life, and Greek mythology was its primary source of inspiration.

♦ **THE MEDICI THEATER IN THE UFFIZI**
Mounting theatrical performances in official government buildings was a common practice in Renaissance Italy, especially in Florence, where in 1584 the architect Bernardo Buontalenti transformed a great hall of the Uffizi into a theater.

♦ *ORPHEUS AND EURYDICE*
With the sound of his lyre, Orpheus was able to bring trees to life and to tame savage beasts. Legend has it that the Thracian singer traveled to Hades to bring back to life his wife, Eurydice, who had been killed by a serpent. The gods of the underworld, moved by Orpheus's song, returned Eurydice to him—provided he not look at her until after they left the underworld. Orpheus, though, was not true to his word; he turned and looked at his wife, and lost her once again. The symbol of song and poetry, Orpheus was a favorite subject from the very dawn of opera. Two members of the Camerata, Caccini and Peri, took up the challenge of this theme. Peri, in contrast to earlier (and later) authors, told the tale with a happy ending. Above, the frontispiece of the original edition of Peri's score.

THE PERFORMANCE OF *EURIDICE*
The very first opera in history had its premiere on October 6, 1600, in the Pitti Palace, the Grand Duke of Tuscany's residence, where a select audience celebrated the marriage of Maria de' Medici to Henri IV of France.

♦ **JACOPO PERI**
(1561–1633)
Before composing *Euridice*, he wrote music for *Dafne*, now lost.

♦ **OTTAVIO RINUCCINI**
(1563–1621)
A Florentine aristocrat, he wrote the poetry Peri set to music.

♦ **MARIA DE' MEDICI**
(1575–1642)
The daughter of Francesco I, Grand Duke of Tuscany, she became queen of France and a powerful regent.

♦ **PITTI PALACE**
In contrast to the current façade, the façade from 1600 displayed the original (fifteenth-century) proportions typical of the grand, civic architectural style born in Renaissance Florence.

♦ **THE CARDINAL**
It was Ferdinando de' Medici who celebrated the marriage of Maria to Henri IV, not actually present for the ceremony, but represented by a courtier.

♦ **GIULIO CACCINI**
(1550–1618)
He sang and played the viol. One of Peri's rivals, and the author of his own *Euridice*, he nevertheless took part in the wedding festivities.

♦ **EMILIO DE' CAVALIER**
(1550–1602)
He supervised the musical activities at the Grand Duke of Tuscany's court.

♦ **GIOVANNI DE' BARDI**
(1534–1612)
His *palazzo* was the meeting place for the Camerata, which explored the need for monodic song in musical theater.

RECITAR CANTANDO
("Acting through song")
The musicians and men of letters who made up the Camerata insisted on the need for monodic (or single-voiced) music, which allowed the text to be enhanced by music instead of obscured by it, as happened with polyphonic (or many-voiced) music. These ideas had been propounded by Vincenzo Galilei (1520–1591) in his *Dialogo della musica antica et moderna* (1581), which proposed a return to the equality of text and music characteristic of ancient times. Above, a set design by Bernardo Buontalenti.

♦ **GABRIELLO CHAIBRERA**
(1552–1638)
His poetry was set to music by many composers.

♦ **COUNT JACOPO CORSI**
The performance of *Euridice* was his wedding present to the bride and groom.

VENICE

While *melodramma* was born as an exclusive, courtly entertainment, its popularity soon led to the construction of specialized theaters that were open to the public. The first opera house was built in the first half of the seventeenth century in Venice, which was to become the capital of this new form of theater. The audience no longer consisted of courtiers, but of anyone who was able to pay for a ticket. The boxes were reserved for noble subscribers; standing room, in the orchestra, was sold on an evening-by-evening basis. When the opera was not sold out, the noisy, enthusiastic gondoliers of Venice were invited to attend. The composer Claudio Monteverdi spent the last years of his life in these surroundings.

♦ **CLAUDIO MONTEVERDI**
Born in Cremona in 1567, he played the viol, sang, and served as chorus master at the court of the Gonzagas in Mantova. He also composed numerous madrigals, some of which have a strong theatrical orientation: the *Combattimento di Tancredi e Clorinda*, for example, from his eighth book of *Madrigali guerrieri et amorosi*, and inspired by Torquato Tasso's epic poem *Jerusalem Delivered*. His *Orfeo*, a tale set to music with a text by Alessandro Striggio, was staged in Mantova in 1607. In 1608, Monteverdi created for the Gonzaga court *Arianna*, a setting of Ottavio Rinuccini's tragedy, whose music (with the exception of Ariadne's *Lamento*) is now lost. Monteverdi spent the last years of his life on operatic undertakings, composing *Il ritorno di Ulisse in patria* and *L'incoronazione di Poppea*. Both were performed in Venice, where Monteverdi died in 1643. Above, his portrait.

♦ **BUSENELLO**
Gian Francesco Busenello (1598–1659) wrote the libretto for *L'incoronazione di Poppea*, an opera with a particularly rich range of styles.

MONTEVERDI'S WORKSHOP
Claudio Monteverdi and his colleagues at work in the hall of a Venetian *palazzo*. As in a painter's workshop, the musicians worked as a team, each making his own individual contribution to *L'incoronazione di Poppea*.

♦ **APPRENTICES**
Younger musicians helped the seventy-five-year-old Monteverdi to compose certain portions of the opera.

♦ **INSTRUMENTS**
The theorbo and the *chitarrone* were used to accompany the singers.

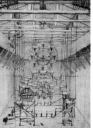

♦ *L'INCORONAZIONE DI POPPEA*
Monteverdi's last opera, first performed in Venice in 1643. Above, Graham Vick's 1992 production for Bologna's *Teatro comunale*.

♦ **OPERA IN VENICE**
"Public" opera was born in 1637, with the opening of the Teatro di San Cassiano. Audience members purchased a ticket to gain entry to the theater. Impresarios and theater owners organized seasons to coincide with Carnival (the feast preceding Lent); two new operas were presented, both of which might be repeated up to thirty times. The libretto was printed, while the score usually remained in manuscript form, and could be modified at the discretion of singers and instrumentalists. Other important composers: Francesco Cavalli (1602–1676), one of Monteverdi's pupils; Pietro Andrea Ziani (1620–1684); and Giovanni Legrenzi (1626–1690), all of whom generally focused on mythological subjects. Above, an etching of Legrenzi's opera *Germanico sul Reno* (1676).

♦ **THE LIBRARY**
Among the sources for the libretto of *L'incoronazione di Poppea*, which portrays events from the history of the Roman empire, are passages from the *Annals* by Tacitus, a Roman historian, which tell of the rise to power by Poppea, the emperor Nero's mistress.

♦ **FRANCESCO CAVALLI**
He was Monteverdi's most gifted pupil, the composer of numerous operas on mythological and amorous subjects.

♦ **MONTEVERDI**
In the last years of his life, he explored music's capacity for vividly portraying human personalities and passions.

EUROPE

Dramma per musica spread from Venice not only to other Italian cities, but also to the rest of Europe. In the second half of the seventeenth century, its developments paralleled those of instrumental music. Italian opera was the standard, alongside of which specific national forms sprang up, as in England. In France, the absolute monarch Louis XIV supported a highly original fusion of song and music: dance was the central element of *tragédie lyrique*, the successful innovation of Jean-Baptiste Lully. A tireless organizer of sumptuous productions, Lully brought to lyric drama the characteristics of great French seventeenth-century spoken dramas.

♦ **TRAGÉDIE LYRIQUE**
Louis XIV's France was an extraordinary time for theater that saw the emergence of great dramatists and playwrights: Pierre Corneille (1606–1684), Molière (1622–1673), and Jean Racine (1639–1699), whose works were inspired by classical precepts and observed rigorous principles of equilibrium, authenticity, and decorum. The lyric dramas of Jean-Baptiste Lully (1632–1687) (above, portrait) followed the same set of rules, and he often collaborated with Molière himself. Lully created the French version of *dramma per musica*, the *tragédie lyrique*, composing fourteen operas for the court of Versailles and the Académie des Opéras in Paris. Lully's operas called for intermezzos and dances in every act (of which there were generally five). The subjects of his most celebrated works were mythological: *Alceste*, *Thésée*, *Bellérophon*, *Amadis*, and *Armide*.

VERSAILLES
On the outskirts of Paris, the sumptuous palace built by Louis XIV was the main site of French courtly life, and of the theatrical productions in which the king himself often participated.

♦ **LULLY**
A native of Florence, his real name was Giovan Battista Lulli. He won the favor of the Sun King, for whom he organized operatic productions.

♦ **DANCERS**
From the 1600s to the 1800s, dance was a fundamental component of French opera.

♦ **MUSICIANS**
Louis XIV allowed Lully to advance instrumental music by financing the largest orchestra of the age, the *Grande Bande des violons du Roi*.

♦ **DIDO AND AENEAS**
This opera by Henry Purcell (premiered in London in 1689) tells of the tragic love of Queen Dido for the hero Aeneas, who landed in Carthage in the course of his wanderings throughout the Mediterranean. At left, a sketch for the 1940 production at the Maggio Musicale Fiorentino.

♦ **EUROPEAN OPERA IN THE 1600s**
Italian opera had the greatest impact in the southern reaches of German-speaking areas: Salzburg, Prague, Munich, and Vienna. The English cultivated a unique form of opera: an entertainment during which dance, song, and instrumental music accompanied stagings of historical and mythological dramas. This theatrical genre, in which music generally provided commentary on mimed action, was known as the masque. Henry Purcell (1659–1695; above, portrait) stood out among English composers. In addition to a great variety of theatrical music, he wrote a brief opera in a prologue and three acts, *Dido and Aeneas*. In Spain, opera initially won little favor, hampered as it was by a local art form, the *zarzuela*, in which music and spoken dialogue alternated.

♦ **LOUIS XIV**
He crafted his public image with immense care, and was often depicted on stage in various allegorical guises.

Singers

Each different phase of operatic history, with its specific styles and genres, has favored certain types of singers and come to be identified with particular vocal registers. Differences among singers are established first of all by the extension of their voices, which can range from the extreme high notes sung by sopranos and tenors to the low notes produced only by baritones and basses. Differences in timbre and in style of singing are also key factors in distinguishing one type of voice from another.

VOCAL REGISTERS
The drawing shows the vocal range of different singers. Range is determined by how low and how high the voice can reach.

♦ **COUNTERTENOR**
Today, the countertenor usually sings the roles created by *castrati* or by female singers in baroque operas, including the title role in Georg Friedrich Händel's *Julius Caesar* (*Giulio Cesare*) (1724).

♦ **TENOR**
The tenor generally stars in the great Romantic operas of the nineteenth century, which require vocal power and athleticism. The operatic tenor par excellence: Manrico in *Il trovatore* (1853) by Giuseppe Verdi.

♦ **BARITONE**
This deeper voice is characteristic of many Mozartian heroes, and often portrays the heroic tenor's rival. An emblematic baritone: Mephistopheles in *Faust* (1859) by Charles Gounod.

♦ **BASS**
The gallery of bass roles varies greatly, from the comic characters of *opera buffa* to grand or wise old men such as Gurnemanz in *Parsifal* (1882) by Richard Wagner.

♦ **COLORATURA SOPRANO**
This is a very light voice, but capable of great virtuosity and of singing extremely high notes. The coloratura is the ideal interpreter of the title role in Gaetano Donizetti's *Lucia di Lammermoor* (1835).

♦ **LYRIC SOPRANO**
This category encompasses many types of voices and styles of singing, and generally designates artists with a rich, lovely timbre. Lyrics can perform the title role in Giacomo Puccini's *Madame Butterfly* (1904).

♦ **DRAMATIC SOPRANO**
The dramatic soprano has a powerful lower register. This category includes the large voices needed for German opera of the late 1800s (Richard Wagner) and for the title role in *Elektra* (1909) by Richard Strauss.

♦ **MEZZO SOPRANO AND CONTRALTO**
They have a similar range, though contraltos generally offer richer tone. Either voice type can take on the title role in Gioacchino Rossini's *La Cenerentola* (1817).

SPLENDORS OF *BEL CANTO*

Dramma per musica became definitively established with the rise of singers who were widely hailed as *divi* (gods and goddesses). By the end of the seventeenth century, famous singers were opera's greatest attraction. Many of these artists were *castrati,* who took on both male and female operatic roles. The most famous *castrati* became known by their stage names, such as Senesino and Farinelli. The time known as the age of *bel canto* (literally, "beautiful singing") coincided with the career of a great musician, Georg Friedrich Händel, whose operas consist primarily of arias.

♦ **HÄNDEL**
The greatest operatic composer of the early seventeenth century was Georg Friedrich Händel (1685–1759; portrait, above). A native of Halle, in Saxony, he traveled to Italy, where he composed operas in Florence, Rome, and Venice. He served as *kapellmeister* in Hanover before moving in 1710 to London, where he was nominated director of the Royal Academy of Music. His vast repertoire includes sacred oratorios, *concerti grossi,* and his celebrated orchestral suite known as *Water Music* (1715–1717). Händel wrote more than forty operas, for the most part in Italian and on mythological subjects. Among his masterpieces: *Agrippina* (Venice, 1709); *Giulio Cesare in Egitto, Tamerlano* (London, 1724); *Rodelinda* (1725); *Alcina* (1735); *Xerxes* (1738). As is often the case in *bel canto*, the solo numbers in Händel's operas have a greater importance than the duets, choruses, and descriptive overtures.

IDOLS
Singers bewitched audiences with their spectacular virtuoso style, utterly devoid of any concern for realism.

♦ **DIVAS**
Singers provoked delirium and fainting spells. Interest in the baroque complexity of Venetian *melodramma* began to wane. Attention was focused entirely on the singer, his aria, and his improvised ornamentation. Sets were relatively simple, since impresarios preferred to spend money on the *divi* and their elaborate costumes.

♦ **THE AUDIENCE**
The virtuosity of star singers became the main attraction for opera audiences.

♦ **THE ORCHESTRA**
The orchestral accompaniment for arias often featured one or more solo instruments in "dialogue" with the voice.

♦ **Senesino**
Francesco Bernardi, known as Senesino (c. 1680–c. 1750), performed in several *opere serie* by Händel that were performed in London. Above, a print showing the *castrato's* arrival in England.

♦ **Castrati**
Starting in the fifteenth century, there arose the barbarous custom of castrating prepubescent boys who had good singing voices and sure intonation. The absence of sexual hormones favored the development of the vocal range, which could encompass the soprano, contralto, tenor, and even bass registers. During the fifteenth century, *castrati*, who had more powerful and agile voices than women, were first called upon to replace female voices in church choruses, where women were not allowed. Throughout the age of *bel canto*, the vogue for *castrati*, which had its origin in Italy, led to the habit of adding or substituting entire arias without regard for dramatic appropriateness. Above, a portrait of Carlo Broschi, known as Farinelli.

♦ **Farinelli**
His real name was Carlo Broschi (1705–1782). A male soprano, the *castrato* Farinelli had an exceptional vocal range, which helped make him the most famous singer in the history of opera.

Two men of letters—Apostolo Zeno (1668–1750) and Pietro Metastasio (1698–1782; portrait, above)—established the canons of *opera seria*, stripping it of comic "contamination" and of baroque intricacies, as well. It was Metastasio who refined the new dramatic conventions that would remain in place until the early nineteenth century. His texts, including *L'Olimpiade*, *La clemenza di Tito*, and *Didone abbandonata*, were frequently set to music by several different composers. The outstanding characteristic of Metastasian drama is the variety of scenes in which the action is set. Nearly every scene concludes with an aria, whose forms and characteristics vary according to the emotion dominating the character at that moment in the drama.

GENRES

At the beginning of the eighteenth century, *opera seria* and *opera buffa* were the two types of lyric drama, both with a strong Italian influence. Heroes, knights, and mythological characters were the protagonists of *opera seria,* which tended to represent an ideal, stylized world. *Opera buffa* had it origins in the comic performances that took place during the two intermezzos of the three acts of *opera seria*. The subjects of *opera buffa* were generally from the everyday world, and thus quick to win the favor of audiences, who appreciated their more realistic qualities. *Opera seria* evolved thanks to the poet Metastasio, while the composer Pergolesi helped make *opera buffa* a success.

NAPLES
The Neapolitan school of opera was at the avant-garde of Europe in the eighteenth century. *Opera seria* interpreters rehearse along with those of the *opera buffa,* who will take the stage during the intermezzos of their colleague's performance.

♦ THE *OPERA BUFFA* SOPRANO
Those performing *opera buffa* must have real theatrical flair in order to bring out the comedy of the situations.

♦ THE *OPERA SERIA* SOPRANO
Those performing *opera seria* need to show great virtuosity as singers.

♦ THE MAESTRO DI MUSICA
The *maestro* was often called upon to alter the score, at the request of performers.

♦ **PERGOLESI AND THE NEAPOLITAN SCHOOL**
Giovan Battista Pergolesi (1710–1736; portrait, above) was the greatest representative of the Neapolitan school. The artistic heir of Alessandro Scarlatti (1660–1725), he composed *La serva padrona,* which premiered in Naples in 1733 during the intermezzos of the *opera seria, Il prigionier superbo.* As time went on, these intermezzos began to win greater favor than the opera that contained them, which came as a surprise to Pergolesi, a master of melody. Among his finest scores: *L'Olimpiade* and *Lo frate 'nam-morato,* in Neapolitan dialect. Niccolò Piccinni, Giovanni Paisiello, and Domenico Cimarosa were among Pergolesi's followers; they influenced many generations of musicians, including Mozart himself.

♦ **CARICATURES**
Singers and their caprices were ridiculed by Benedetto Marcello in his satire, *Il teatro alla moda,* from 1720. Above, a caricature of Niccolò Grimaldi, known as Nicolino, with Francesca Cuzzoni.

♦ **THE POET AND THE IMPRESARIO**
New professionals came to the fore in the world of opera. In the eighteenth century, men of letters transformed the writing of librettos into a craft, while impresarios focused on hiring singers and instrumentalists.

THE ELEMENTS OF OPERA

The different elements of an opera determine its musical structure. Such elements are distinct and easily identified in the works of the late eighteenth century, when opera in the Italian style enjoyed its greatest fortune, in Italy and all over Europe. An orchestral selection, the overture, is played before the curtain rises and the dramatic action begins. Various musical "pieces" follow: arias, duets, trios, and so forth, depending on the number of characters on stage at a given time. With time, the structural patterns of opera become ever more elaborate, as in the masterpieces of Mozart. The divisions among the various set pieces tend to disappear in the nineteenth century, when an increasing "fusion" between singers and orchestra, and a greater concern for dramatic realism, made themselves felt.

3. **ARIA** The singer's solo performance, in which he or she expresses a single, dominant emotion. *Carolina's father, Don Geronio, has arranged for Count Robinson to marry Elisetta, his other daughter, and he announces the news to his family.*

1. **OVERTURE** The prelude, performed by the orchestra before the curtain rises and the first act begins. In this case, the opera is *Il matrimonio segreto* by Domenico Cimarosa.

2. **INTRODUCTION** Several voices accompanied by the orchestra, shortly after the curtain rises. *Carolina, the daughter of a rich merchant, has secretly married Paolino, a shop-boy. The young couple meets secretly.*

A "NUMBER" OPERA
The musical structure of Domenico Cimarosa's *Il matrimonio segreto* is made up of many different elements that, scene after scene, advance the action of the opera.

4. CAVATINA This is an aria that serves to introduce a given character. *Upon his arrival, Count Robinson declares that he prefers Carolina, to the dismay of all.*

5. RECITATIVE Between numbers, the action moves forward accompanied by solo harpsichord, which underpins the performers' sung dialogue. *Throwing matters into greater confusion, Geronio's sister Fidalma, who is in love with Paolino, arrives.*

6. FINALE A *concertato* (a "polyphonic" or many-voiced piece for voices and orchestra) closes each act. *Carolina and Paolino have decided to run away. But in the end, Count Robinson intercedes on their behalf, and agrees to marry Elisetta.*

♦ **CIMAROSA** Domenico Cimarosa (1749–1801; above, portrait) composed *Il matrimonio segreto* and seventy other operas, including intermezzos, *drammi giocosi* (semi-serious operas), and *opere serie.* Born near Naples, he traveled to London, Saint Petersburg, Vienna, and Weimar, and was organist in the royal chapel of the Neapolitan court. Among his most important works are *I traci amanti, Le astuzie femminili, Gli Orazi ed i Curiazi,* and the intermezzo *Il maestro di cappella.* His masterwork is *Il matrimonio segreto,* which librettist Giuseppe Bertati (1735–1815) based on a comedy by English authors George Colman and David Garrick, who had themselves been inspired by William Hogarth's cycle of paintings known as *Le mariage à la mode.* The opera premiered at Vienna's Burgtheater in the winter of 1792, and was such a success that the singers performed it again in its entirety as an encore, following a banquet offered by Emperor Leopold II.

GLUCK AND THE "REFORM"

In eighteenth-century Paris, the capital of Enlightenment thought, debates and controversies about opera were all the rage. At mid-century, as a result of the great enthusiasm for Italian *opera buffa* and its realistic nature, the so-called *querelle des bouffons* broke out, which questioned the value of antiquated, state-subsidized French opera. Several decades later, with the arrival of the German musician Christoph Willibald Gluck, Italian *opera seria* was found to be contrived, lacking in realism, and excessively accomodating of singers, their caprices, and their self-indulgent antics.

♦ **CHRISTOPH WILLIBALD GLUCK** (1714–1787) Once a traditionalist, and the author of *opere serie* for theaters throughout Europe, Gluck (portrait, above) then came out in favor of reform and against conventions and the caprices of singers. His operas *Orfeo ed Euridice*, *Alceste*, and *Iphigénie en Tauride* sought to express emotion by creating a balance between poetry and music, and to rediscover the aesthetic harmony of ancient Greek tragedy. Gluck's manifesto on operatic reform appeared in the preface to *Alceste*, written in 1767 by Ranier de' Calzabigi (1714–1795). The overture is directly relevant to the action on stage. Changes of scene are kept to a minimum, in the name of authenticity and of rapid, concise action. As in the ancient world, the chorus plays a leading role. The orchestration does not merely accompany singers, but serves an expressive purpose.

♦ **DENIS DIDEROT** (1713–1784) An author and philosopher, he also wrote on aesthetic and musical matters. He was a defender of Italian opera.

♦ **MELCHIOR GRIMM** (1723–1807) A German intellectual, he spread news of the cultural and political happenings in Paris to the crowned heads of Europe in his

Correspondance littéraire, philosophique et critique (1753–1768). A supporter of Italian *opera buffa* at mid-century, he sided with Gluck in the 1770s.

THE ENCYCLOPÉDIE
Between 1751 and 1772 the twenty-eight volumes of the *Encyclopédie* were published under the direction of Diderot and d'Alembert. The *Encyclopédie* served to counter dogmatism, superstition, and intolerance.

♦ IPHIGÉNIE
The subject for *Iphigénie en Tauride* was taken from Euripides's drama. Gluck's lyric drama premiered in Paris in 1779 in direct competition with an opera of the same name by Niccolò Piccinni. Above, a scene from the production at the 1981 Maggio Musicale Fiorentino.

♦ JEAN-PHILIPPE RAMEAU
After Lully's *tragédie en musique,* Jean-Philippe Rameau (1683–1764) brought about the next major change in eighteenth-century French opera, expanding the confines of the repertory with such works as *Hippolyte et Aricie* (1733), *Les Indes galantes* (1735), and *Zoroastre* (1749). Sensitive to opera's solemn aspects, Rameau was also involved in the debates that pitted Italian opera against French opera in the celebrated *querelle des bouffons*, which arose from the extraordinary success in Paris of Pergolesi's *La serva padrona*. In his *Lettre sur la musique française* (1752), Jean-Jacques Rousseau (1712–1778) argued for the greater melodiousness of the Italian language. Above, a scene from Rameau's *Dardanus* (1739).

♦ THEATER
The figures in the *Encyclopédie* represented the first attempt to provide scientific illustrations, disseminating information from every branch of knowledge.

♦ ALGAROTTI
The *Saggio sopra l'opera per musica* (1755) by Francesco Algarotti (1712–1764) anticipated the spirit of Gluck's reform.

MOZART

♦ **HIS LIFE**
Wolfgang Amadeus
Mozart (1756–1791)
was a child prodigy
in all forms of music,
including opera. A
native of Salzburg,
Mozart composed
his first opera,
Bastien et Bastienne,
at the age of 12, and
at 18 composed
Mitridate, re di Ponto,
an *opera seria.*
Between 1781 and
1791, this musical
genius created
a number of
masterworks that
are treasured to this
day, starting with
Idomeneo, re di Creta,
an *opera seria* from
1781, and *The
Abduction from the
Seraglio,* a German-
language *singspiel*
(alternating music
and spoken dialogue)
from 1782. Mozart's
collaboration with
librettist Lorenzo Da
Ponte (1749–1838)
began with *The
Marriage of Figaro,*
based on the comedy
by Beaumarchais, in
1786; Da Ponte also
wrote the libretti for
Don Giovanni (1787),
a *dramma giocoso,*
and *Così fan tutte*
(1790), an *opera
buffa.* The *opera
seria La clemenza
di Tito* and the
*singspiel Die
Zauberflöte (The
Magic Flute),* both
from 1791, were
written several
months before
Mozart's death.
Above, Papageno's
costume from
The Magic Flute.

Wolfgang Amadeus Mozart composed operas in
every genre, showing an extraordinary theatrical
gift even in childhood. But his contribution to the
history of opera is not limited to his familiarity with
the traditional musical languages he inherited.
Mozart was a genius because he renewed existing
forms (*opera seria, dramma buffo*), filling them
with poignant human values. With *Die Entführung
aus dem Serail (The Abduction from the Seraglio),*
Mozart founded German national opera. In *Le nozze
di Figaro (The Marriage of Figaro),* he offered a
moving exploration of human emotions. And in
Don Giovanni, the story of an unrepentant libertine,
he created an incomparably haunting drama.

♦ **DON GIOVANNI**
Mozart's most
famous opera, a
combination of
tragedy and
farce, tells the
story of a
seducer and
murderer.

♦ **DA PONTE**
The greatest
librettist of the late
eighteenth century,
he lived in Vienna
from 1781 to 1791
and also wrote
librettos for Salieri
and Martini.

♦ **ANTONIO SALIERI**
(1750–1825)
An Italian
musician, Salieri
was *kapellmeister*
at the Viennese
court and the
author of about
forty operas.

THE MARRIAGE OF FIGARO
The Marriage of Figaro had its premiere
on May 1, 1786 at the Burgtheater
in Vienna. Emperor Josef II greeted
Mozart and his singers after the
performance.

♦ **MOZART**
After conducting
the opera's
premiere from
the harpsichord,
he received
the courtiers.

♦ **THE EMPEROR**
Josef II
(1741–1790)
was Mozart's
patron, though
often baffled by
the complexity
and originality
of his scores.

♦ **COURTIERS**
The court
musicians who
surrounded
and advised the
monarch often
determined the
the ultimate
fortune of a
composer.

♦ **KOSTANZE
WEBER**
She was Mozart's
wife, and was
from a long line
of musicians.

ROSSINI

In the early years of the nineteenth century, the European operatic scene was dominated by Gioacchino Rossini. Acutely sensitive to his public and with strong theatrical gifts, Rossini worked tirelessly during the early years of his career. In eight years—from 1815 to 1823—he composed twenty operas. He then spent many unproductive years enjoying the fruits of his enormous fame and prestige. Rossini's training, strongly influenced by German music, endowed him with a flair for brilliant orchestration. The result was the "Rossini crescendo": a dizzying increase in musical pace and intensity. Rossini's captivating overtures have an irresistible effect on audiences.

♦ HIS LIFE
Born in Pesaro in 1792, Gioacchino Rossini (above, a drawing) studied at the Liceo Musicale in Bologna and made his debut with *La cambiale di matrimonio* at Venice's Teatro San Moise in 1810. After composing several *farse* (short comic operas), Rossini established himself as a composer of tragic opera with *Tancredi*, and of *opera buffa* with *L'italiana in Algeri*, both of which premiered in Venice in 1813. His career also flourished in Naples, where the impresario Domenico Barbaja commissioned him to write tragic operas for the Teatro San Carlo. Rossini married the soprano Isabella Colbran, for whom he had written *Elisabetta regina d'Inghilterra*, *Armida*, *La donna del lago*, and *Semiramide*, which was staged in Venice in 1823. Rossini then moved to Paris, where *William Tell* (*Guillaume Tell*), which premiered at the Opéra in 1829, marked his farewell to the theater. Rich and showered with honors, he retired to his villa in Passy, where he died in 1868.

ROMAN TRIUMPHS
Outside the theater, delirious audience members and singers still in costume carried Rossini in triumph from his home. The success of his comic opera *Il barbiere di Siviglia* (*The Barber of Seville*), despite its mixed initial reception, was to prove enduring.

♦ ROSSINI
Rossini's operas won him the admiration of the public and of writers like Stendhal who, enraptured by Rossini's genius, wrote his biography.

♦ TENOR
Count Almaviva is in love with Rosina. He disguises himself as Lindoro, a poor student, to test the young woman's sincerity.

♦ MUSICIANS
The scoring for orchestra is particularly brilliant in all of Rossini's operas.

♦ BASS
Don Basilio, Figaro's nemesis, tries to convince Don Bartolo to slander Count Almaviva.

♦ BASS
Don Bartolo, Rosina's guardian, keeps her hidden at home, hoping to marry her himself and obtain her large dowry.

♦ CONTRALTO
Rosina, Don Bartolo's ward, is not allowed to leave the house. But she manages to meet her Lindoro just the same.

♦ **WILLIAM TELL**
Rossini's last operatic work,
composed for the Paris Opéra
in 1829, tells the story of the Swiss
national hero who came to represent
the Romantic desire for liberty.
Above, the frontispiece of the opera.

♦ **ISABELLA
COLBRAN**
Rossini composed
many of his great-
est works for this
celebrated singer.
She was the com-
poser's first wife.

♦ **BARITONE**
Figaro does all
he can to help
Count Almaviva,
his former
master, win the
love of Rosina.

THE PUBLIC AND IMPRESARIOS

In the early nineteenth century, opera was a popular form of entertainment. Organizing an opera season involved not only composers and singers, but many other figures, including impresarios. Their primary objective was to stage new operas by fashionable composers (including Vincenzo Bellini, the young Sicilian), to be interpreted by the most beloved singers of the time. These included Giuditta Pasta, the most illustrious and imaginative interpreter of Bellini's operas.

THE PREMIERE AT LA SCALA
Vincenzo Bellini's *Norma* opened the season at Milan's Teatro alla Scala on December 26, 1831. A crowd of admirers greeted the leading soprano, Giuditta Pasta.

♦ SHOPS
Theater neighborhoods attracted not only composers and singers, but also instrument makers and music publishers, who sold librettos and piano scores to fans, encouraging performances at home.

♦ FANS
Audiences crowded theaters of the time to applaud the divas of *bel canto*. Their offerings included bouquets of flowers, sonnets, and other poems written in honor of the singers.

♦ **AT LA SCALA**
One of the great "temples" of opera, La Scala was designed by the architect Giuseppe Piermarini (1734–1808) and opened in 1778. Its stage has seen the premieres of many works by Rossini, Bellini, Donizetti, and Verdi.

♦ **NORMA**
Vincenzo Bellini's masterpiece tells the story of a Druid priestess secretly in love with a Roman general. At left, a set design for a production from 1898–1899.

♦ **BELLINI**
The Sicilian Vincenzo Bellini (1801–1835; portrait, above) composed works for Milan and Venice after completing his studies in Naples. He wrote relatively few operas compared with his contemporaries, which allowed him to deepen his poetic vein, inspired by the ideals of Romanticism, already apparent in *Il pirata* (1827). The composer of *I Capuleti ed i Montecchi* and *La sonnambula*, Bellini found in Giuditta Pasta, the most acclaimed singer of the time, the ideal interpreter for *Norma*, which opened the La Scala season in December 1831. He was invited to Paris to write an opera for the Théâtre Italien, and chose a drama set in England at the time of the wars between the followers of Cromwell and the Stuarts: *I puritani*. Bellini died just a few months after the great triumph of this opera.

♦ **GIUDITTA PASTA** (1797–1865)
She created the title role in *Norma* and was one of the goddesses of *bel canto*. Bellini also wrote *La sonnambula* for her.

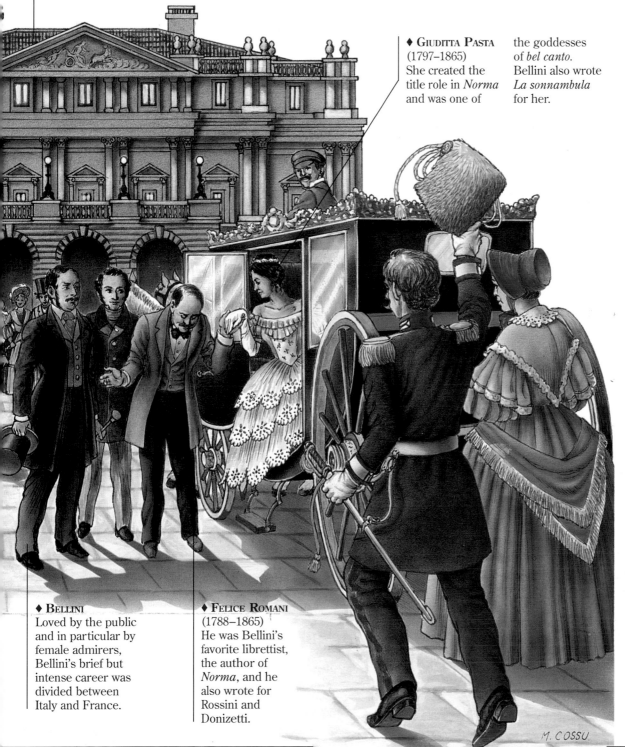

♦ **BELLINI**
Loved by the public and in particular by female admirers, Bellini's brief but intense career was divided between Italy and France.

♦ **FELICE ROMANI** (1788–1865)
He was Bellini's favorite librettist, the author of *Norma*, and he also wrote for Rossini and Donizetti.

M. COSSU.

ROMANTICISM

The Romantic era witnessed a new evolution in operatic subjects, drawn for the first time from contemporary narrative and fantastic tales. A new feeling for nature sprang up, which was reflected in the newly diverse range of operatic themes. Bellini, Donizetti, and other composers focused their works on tormented female characters, victims of situations that drive them to madness or death. In Germany, opera often explored the supernatural world. With Beethoven's *Fidelio*, opera became a hymn to liberty and to the destruction of tyranny's chains.

♦ **DONIZETTI**
Gaetano Donizetti (portrait, above) was born in Bergamo in 1797 to a poor family. He attended the music school founded by Giovanni Simone Mayr, who took note of his young pupil's great gifts and sent him to Bologna to study counterpoint. Donizetti's frenetic production of operas began in 1816: he composed both comic and serious works. His masterpieces belong to his later period: *Anna Bolena,* with a libretto by Felice Romani, triumphed in 1830 at the Teatro Carcano of Milan; two years later, *L'elisir d'amore* was staged at La Scala; and the following year, *Lucrezia Borgia* premiered, also at La Scala. Donizetti wrote *Lucia di Lammermoor* (1835) for the Teatro San Carlo in Naples. He traveled constantly between Italy and France, and composed his final masterwork, *Don Pasquale* (1843), for Paris. Ill and exhausted, he died in 1848 in the city of his birth.

MAD SCENE
The mad scene is the dramatic climax of Donizetti's *Lucia di Lammermoor.* Lucia, sad and deranged, makes her appearance on stage.

♦ **THE CASTLE**
Donizetti's opera, drawn from a famous and popular novel by Sir Walter Scott, is set in Scotland.

♦ **LUCIA**
Lucia swore undying love for Edgardo, who was from an enemy clan. When forced to marry another man, she stabs her bridegroom in a final gesture of desperation.

♦ **ENRICO**
Lucia's brother belongs to the Ashton family, a noble Scottish clan.

♦ **THE WOODS**
The feeling for nature that dominates Romantic poetics also finds expression in the world of opera.

♦ **THE CEMETERY**
Gothic tales, filled with ghosts and supernatural elements, form the basis for many Romantic operas.

♦ **THE CHORUS**
The chorus witnesses and comments on the drama's unfolding events.

♦ **ROMANTIC OPERA**
In Germany, the Romantic movement first found expression in symphonic and chamber music, and soon thereafter in musical theater. Ludwig van Beethoven (1770–1827) wrote a single opera, *Fidelio* (1805), a hymn to liberty and to universal solidarity. This was followed by *Undine* by author and composer E.T.A. Hoffmann (1776–1822), and *Faust* by Louis Spohr (1784–1859). But it was Carl Maria von Weber (1786–1826) who gave Romantic opera its novel, fundamental impulse. His masterpiece, *Der Freischütz* (1821; above, a sketch), combined the new feeling for nature with a disturbing, "demonic" sensibility. Other works by Weber include *Euryanthe* and *Oberon*.

THE LIBRETTO

The term "libretto" (literally, "little book"), used to designate the text of an opera, defines not only the action itself (usually set forth in verse), but also the volume published for spectators to read before the performance, to familiarize themselves with the story of the opera. Until the end of the eighteenth century, librettos consisted of a series of arias, duets, and ensembles that were written according to strict metrical conventions (those considered easiest to sing). Librettists at first drew their subjects from ancient theater, and then, in the nineteenth century, from the dramas of their contemporaries and from the new historical novel, adapting plots and characters to the formal requirements of opera and to public taste.

♦ **LIBRETTISTS**
In the early days of opera, librettists were poets and men of letters who lived at court. With time, though, they acquired a separate professional status. Pietro Metastasio was imperial poet at the Viennese court, and devoted himself exclusively to writing librettos, which were often set by more than one composer. Mozart and Da Ponte, in contrast, had a more exclusive relationship. Felice Romani (1788–1865) and Francesco Maria Piave (1810–1876), who worked with Verdi, and Luigi Illica, Puccini's librettist, were especially prolific. Wagner was the first major musician to write the texts of his own operas. In the twentieth century, the practice of setting "legitimate" theatrical texts to music (as in the case of Debussy and Berg) became increasingly common. Above, a painting by Auguste Renoir (1874) showing a theater box (London, Courtauld Institute).

♦ **BOXES**
In the nineteenth century, theater boxes often belonged to noble or wealthy families, who would call on each other during the performance.

LORENZO DA PONTE
(1749–1838)
This librettist from Venice enjoyed an adventurous, licentious lifestyle, collaborated with the most important composers of his time, and served as poet for the imperial theaters in Vienna. His greatest strengths as a librettist were the psychological depth of his characters and the rapid, lively nature of his verses.

THE THEATER
The theater was a meeting place for audiences, who came not only to see the performance but also to make social calls. The audience itself, then, was one of the evening's principal attractions, and the theater was left illuminated during the performance until the end of the nineteenth century.

♦ **LA TRAVIATA**
Composed in 1853 by Verdi, to a libretto by Francesco Maria Piave, this opera was drawn from a play by Alexandre Dumas *fils* that depicted contemporary society.

♦ **HUGO VON HOFMANNSTHAL**
(1874–1929)
This Austrian poet wrote the librettos for some of Richard Strauss's greatest operas, starting with *Der Rosenkavalier* (1911), which was inspired by Italian *opera buffa*. Their collaboration continued with *Ariadne auf Naxos* (1916) and *Die Frau ohne Schatten* (1919), drawn from myth and fable.

♦ **THE LIBRETTO**
From the earliest days of opera, it was customary to print the text of an opera and distribute it to the public.

GRAND-OPÉRA

Sumptuous sets, elaborate choreography, intricate plots, and historical subjects were the essential ingredients of French *grand-opéra* from about 1830 on. The *grand-opéra,* not surprisingly, was of epic proportions and length. Gioacchino Rossini, Giuseppe Verdi, and Richard Wagner all wrote operas in this genre. Its greatest exponent, though, was Giacomo Meyerbeer, who wrote the most popular works in this form, which went forth from the Académie Royale de Musique in Paris to conquer the stages of the operatic world.

♦ **PARISIAN SOCIETY**
Grand-opéra was the center not only of musical life, but of all of Parisian society. The subjects for these elaborate spectacles were often chosen by Eugène Scribe (1791–1861), who wrote most of the librettos for Giacomo Meyerbeer (1791–1864), including *Robert le diable, Les Hugenots,* and *Le prophète,* which combined music, dance, and majestic choral scenes, and were inspired by historical events like the religious wars of the seventeenth century. The French composer Daniel Auber (1782–1871), author of *La muette de Portici,* was also among the founders of *grand-opéra.* For the very first time, newspapers devoted extensive coverage to the preparations for each new production, creating an atmosphere of great anticipation among the public. Above, the Paris Opéra in 1874.

THE OPÉRA
The Académie Royale de Musique in Paris—also known as the Opéra—commissioned operas and other works from such composers as Rossini, Donizetti, and Verdi.

♦ **SET DESIGNERS**
Grand-opéra gave new life to the craft of set design, with its demands for both realism and spectacular theatrical effects.

♦ **BALZAC**
Honoré de Balzac (1799–1850), the great realist, wrote *La comédie humaine.* A passionate opera fan and admirer of Rossini, he wrote a number of novels and tales on operatic subjects.

♦ **LOUIS VERON** (1798–1867) He was the powerful director of the Opéra from 1831 to 1835.

♦ **THE TENOR DUPREZ**
The innovative singing style of Gilbert-Louis Duprez (1806–1896) marked a new era in operatic history.

♦ **THE *DO DI PETTO***
The tenor Gilbert-Louis Duprez (1806–1896) introduced the *do di petto* during the Italian premiere of Rossini's *William Tell,* which took place in Lucca in 1831. He sang a full-throated high C, which singers had previously sung in falsetto, introducing a new style of singing characterized by strong, heroic phrasing. Duprez thus established the myth of the modern, Romantic tenor. Above, a costume from *Benvenuto Cellini,* an opera written by Duprez himself. After singing in operas by Rossini and Donizetti, Duprez moved to Paris, where he replaced Adolphe Nourrit (1802–1839) as the favorite tenor at the Opéra, taking on leading roles in the operas of Berlioz and Meyerbeer.

♦ **MEYERBEER AND SCRIBE**
This composer-librettist pair did the most to establish the genre of *grand-opéra* in Paris.

♦ **GAUTIER AND HEINE**
Théophile Gautier (1811–1872), the French man of letters, and Heinrich Heine (1797–1856), the German poet, were passionately involved in the musical and operatic scene in Paris, and wrote numerous journalistic reports.

VERDI

Verdi's operas created a furor among the public. This Italian composer became the undisputed master of opera in the late nineteenth century thanks to the soaring, passionate melodies that abound in his works. The choruses in his operas were transformed into patriotic hymns of the *Risorgimento*, or movement for Italian independence. But it was on the operatic stage and in his music that Verdi brought about the most lasting revolution, in his choice of subjects and librettos and careful attention to stagecraft. The innovative spirit of his music drama often met with disapproval from the censors of the time.

♦ **HIS LIFE**
Giuseppe Verdi (portrait, above) was born in 1813 in Busseto, near Parma. He took private music lessons in Milan, where his earliest operas met with mixed receptions until the triumph of *Nabucco,* his third work for the stage. Between 1839 and 1853, Verdi composed eighteen operas for the theaters of Milan, Venice, and Rome. Thanks to his great fame, with time he grew to depend less and less on impresarios, and was able to compose without haste, and even to rewrite some of his earlier operas. Verdi was invited to create works for Paris and Saint Petersburg; from 1871 on, he was covered with glory, and slowed down the pace of his composing even further. His last work was a comedy, *Falstaff.* Verdi died in Milan in 1901.

♦ **VERDI**
In March 1842, Verdi scored a huge success at La Scala with *Nabucco.* The libretto by Temistocle Solera (1815–1878), drawn from the Bible, tells of the oppression of the Jews by the bloodthirsty king of Babylon.

AT LA SCALA
Verdi began his operatic career in 1839 with *Oberto, conte di San Bonifacio*, and brought it to an end in 1893 with *Falstaff.* In 1855, during a revival of *Nabucco*, the audience expressed its patriotic fervor and disdain for the Austrian invaders with flyers and bouquets.

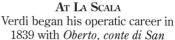

♦ **AUSTRIAN SOLDIERS AND OFFICERS**
When *Nabucco* premiered, Lombardy was part of the Hapsburg empire and Milan was occupied by the Austrian army.

♦ **AN ENTHUSIASTIC PUBLIC**
Verdi was both a musician and a symbol of the *Risorgimento*; the patriots who wrote "Viva Verdi!" on the walls were secretly acclaiming *Vittorio Emanuele Re d'Italia*.

♦ **BOITO AND VERDI**
Arrigo Boito (1842–1918), a poet and musician who had at first sought to "surpass" Verdi, eventually became his collaborator.

♦ **VERDI'S OPERAS**
Verdi's operas rely on concise, essential expressive resources. He chose his subjects cannily, nearly always winning the favor of his audience. After *Nabucco* (1842), Verdi wrote *I Lombardi alla prima crociata* (1843), *Ernani* (1844), and *Macbeth* (1847). Next came his popular masterpieces: *Rigoletto* (1851), *Il trovatore* (1853), and *La traviata* (1853), which offered the novelty of a contemporary subject (above, a sketch for Act III). In *Un ballo in maschera* (1859), Verdi mixed comic and tragic elements. He then took up the challenge of *grand-opéra* with *Les vêpres siciliennes* (1855) and *Don Carlos* (1867). *Aïda* (1871), *Otello* (1887), and *Falstaff* (1893) are his final works for the stage, the last two inspired by Shakespeare and with librettos by Boito. In addition to his operas, Verdi also wrote a *Messa da Requiem* (1874).

♦ **"VA PENSIERO"**
During the *Risorgimento*, Italians heard in the chorus of the Hebrew slaves an anthem of their own oppression.

WAGNER

Wagner's ideal of *Wort-Ton-Drama* (a drama of words and music) broke with the traditional forms of opera in the name of a greater equilibrium among its different elements. The operas inspired by this concept offer an uninterrupted flow of music and action, expressed through a complex harmonic texture. Wagner, who considered himself a poet, playwright, and philosopher in addition to a composer, envisioned a theater that might stage only his attempts to create a universal work of art. Thanks to several wealthy admirers and to King Ludwig II of Bavaria, what might have seemed the mere fancy of an idealist was actually achieved at Bayreuth. Wagner's operas were inspired for the most part by the myths and medieval legends of Germany.

♦ **HIS LIFE**
Richard Wagner (portrait, above) was born in Leipzig in 1813. He studied music on and off, but early on came up with his first plans for an opera, which took form in *Rienzi*, first performed in Dresden in 1842. Wagner moved to Paris, where he did not obtain the great success he sought; he wrote *Der fliegender Holländer* and *Tannhäuser.* He took part in the revolutionary movement in Dresden in 1848 and was forced to take refuge in Zürich without attending the premiere of *Lohengrin* (conducted by Franz Liszt) in Weimar. Wagner worked as a music critic and also wrote his aesthetic manifesto, *The Artwork of the Future* (1849) while drawing up plans for *Der Ring des Niebelungen*, whose composition would be interrupted by *Tristan und Isolde* and *Die Meistersinger.* Wagner wrote *Parsifal* in 1881, and died in Venice in 1883.

♦ **KING LUDWIG II**
The king was one of Wagner's great admirers, supporting the composer (and paying off his debts) from the time he took the throne in 1864, at the age of 18.

♦ **WAGNER**
He wrote the texts for his own operas, in addition to essays on a variety of subjects.

♦ **FRANZ LISZT AND COSIMA LISZT**
The celebrated pianist (1811–1886) was one of Wagner's most ardent supporters. His daughter Cosima (1837–1930) married Wagner and carried on the tradition of the Bayreuth festival.

BAYREUTH
With the help of the architect Brückwald, Wagner created his ideal theater in a small Bavarian town. This unified, contained environment was designed to transform the audience into a community. The different levels of seats were abolished, and it was possible for the first time to darken the hall, creating an unambiguous separation between the performance and the audience.

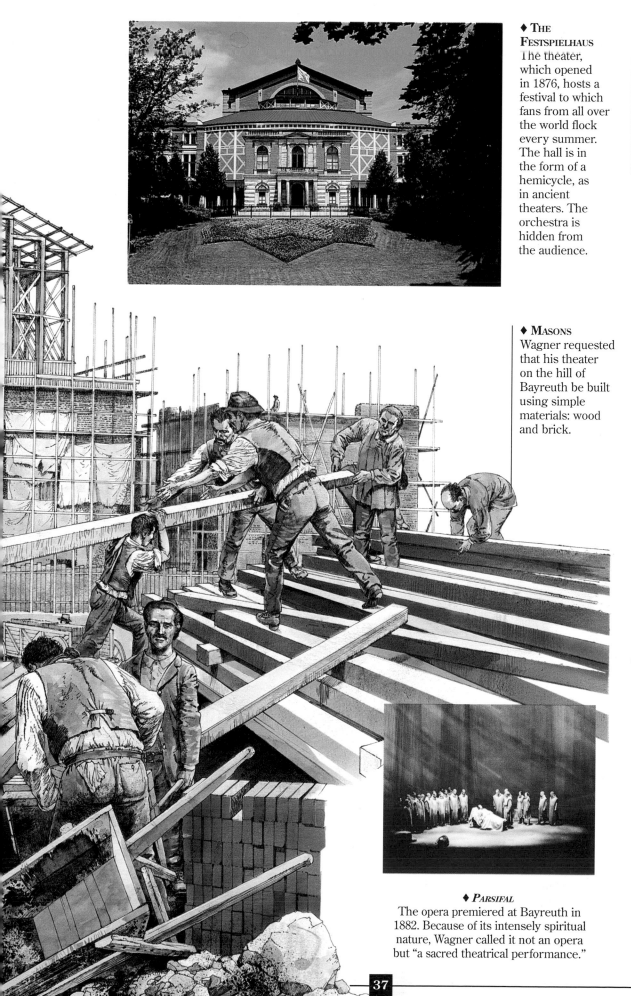

♦ THE FESTSPIELHAUS

The theater, which opened in 1876, hosts a festival to which fans from all over the world flock every summer. The hall is in the form of a hemicycle, as in ancient theaters. The orchestra is hidden from the audience.

♦ *DER RING DES NIEBELUNGEN*

Based on a Germanic epic poem, the *Ring* tells the history of the world through the quest for absolute power that overcomes both gods and heroes, driving them to their downfall. The long creative process that led to the *Ring* (perhaps the longest opera in the history of music) lasted from 1848 to 1874. The tetralogy (a Greek work indicating the four works of which the *Ring* is composed) comprises a prologue, *Das Rheingold*, and three days: *Die Walküre*, *Siegfried*, and *Götterdämmerung*. The cycle in its entirety lasts more than eighteen hours and had its premiere in Bayreuth on August 13 to 17, 1876. Above, H. Hendrich, *Siegfried Battling the Dragon*.

♦ MASONS

Wagner requested that his theater on the hill of Bayreuth be built using simple materials: wood and brick.

♦ *PARSIFAL*

The opera premiered at Bayreuth in 1882. Because of its intensely spiritual nature, Wagner called it not an opera but "a sacred theatrical performance."

THE MYSTIC GULF

The orchestra is, along with the singers, the leading "character" in an opera: it not only accompanies singers, but also introduces the dramatic action, accentuates its development, and evokes the states of mind of the characters interpreted by the singers. For these reasons, composers have always been extremely attentive to the timbres and the instrumental combinations offered by the orchestra. Until the nineteenth century, the number of musicians was relatively small: they occupied the space directly in front of the stage and could be seen by the audience. The orchestra eventually grew to such a degree that it blocked the spectators' view of the stage. It was Richard Wagner who made the orchestra disappear into the "mystic gulf"—the pit in front of the stage that makes the musicians invisible to the audience. Wagner's innovation was eventually adopted by all opera theaters.

THE ORCHESTRA
The number of instruments in the orchestra has varied over the years and grew significantly between the eighteenth and nineteenth centuries. It generally consists of up to 70 musicians, with the strings most often set against the rest of the instruments.

♦ **WOODWINDS**
This family of instruments includes flutes, clarinets, bassoons, and contrabassoons. They were often used in ensembles in the eighteenth century, and in the nineteenth century helped to enhance theatrical moods.

♦ **THE HARP**
A typically Romantic instrument, composers used the harp most often to accompany great melodic outpourings.

♦ **STRINGS**
Strings usually constitute the majority of the orchestra and include first and second violins, violas, cellos, and contrabasses. In operas of the classical age, they generally accompany the melody.

♦ **THE CONDUCTOR**
Until the end of the eighteenth century, the conductor was generally a *maestro concertatore* who sat at the keyboard providing the *basso continuo*. His role has grown in importance over the years with the greater complexity of orchestral scores.

♦ **The orchestra in art**
Edgar Degas, *The Opera Orchestra* (detail), 1868–1869; oil on canvas, 20.8" × 17.7" (53 × 45 cm). Paris, Musée d'Orsay.

♦ **Brass**
Trumpets, trombones, horns, and tubas assume greater importance in orchestras of the Romantic age. Their name is derived from the material from which they are constructed. One particular type of tuba was introduced by Wagner especially for the *Ring*.

♦ **Percussion**
Drums and cymbals were used infrequently, for the most part, until the first half of the nineteenth century.

♦ **The conductor**
The role of the conductor became important only in the early nineteenth century. Before then, small instrumental groups needed only a *concertatore,* who often played harpsichord or first violin at the same time. His job was to indicate tempo and to signal the entrance of the various sections of the orchestra. As scores became more complex and ensembles grew in size, the conductor emerged as an autonomous figure who was responsible for the performance. The baton was introduced in the nineteenth century to make the conductor's indications easier to see. With the passing of time, the conductor emerged as an actual interpreter of the opera, one who could put his own personal stamp on the score he conducted. Above, conductor and composer Gustav Mahler (1860–1911).

THE RUSSIAN SCHOOL

In the nineteenth century, the widespread reawakening of patriotism and the rediscovery of the popular roots of national culture made themselves felt in opera, as well, bringing an end to the phenomenon of a "European" musical language (that had been, in effect, the Italian model since the eighteenth century). The new concern with ethnic identity brought forth numerous national schools within the operatic tradition. The prototypes for the Russian school of opera were the works of Mikhail Glinka, whose style fused elements of international culture and of the Russian musical heritage. The masterworks of Mussorgsky, drawn from the most dramatic pages of Russian history, endowed Russian opera with true artistic autonomy.

♦ **MUSSORGSKY**
Modest Mussorgsky (1839–1881; portrait, above) was born to a family of landowners. In spite of his military career, he was able to continue his musical education. Starting in 1863, he lived in Saint Petersburg among artists and philosophers, and studied music on his own. He drew up sketches for an opera based on *Salammbô*, the historical novel by Gustave Flaubert (1821–1880), though his health continued to decline because of alcoholism and mental illness. In 1871, the Marinski Theater in Saint Petersburg turned down his opera *Boris Godunov,* based on the historical drama by Pushkin. Three years later, a subsequent version of the opera scored a huge success. Mussorgsky died in 1881 without completing his final opera, *Kovanchina,* also inspired by Russian history.

THE CORONATION
On October 1, 1598, a solemn procession accompanied the new Czar Boris across Moscow's Kremlin Square. Mussorgsky offered a faithful reconstruction of the events related in Pushkin's historical drama.

♦ **CZAR BORIS**
(1546–1605) He was ruthless in his pursuit of the throne, which had been left vacant at the end of the sixteenth century.

♦ **EUGENE ONEGIN**
The "lyric scenes" created by Peter Ilyich Tchaikovsky offer glimpses of Russian life in the early nineteenth century. Here, a scene from the 1973 La Scala production.

♦ **THE CATHEDRAL**
The cathedral stands in the central square of Moscow, its bells tolling joyously.

♦ **THE BAYARDS**
The Bayards were the Russian nobles who advised the Czar. Ivan the Terrible had sought to reduce their power.

♦ **PRIESTS**
The patriarch Iov was greatly devoted to Boris and supported his ascension to the throne.

♦ **RUSSIAN OPERA**
Russian opera had its origins in the works of Mikhail Glinka (1804–1857), including *A Life for the Czar* and *Ruslan and Lyudmilla*. There followed *The Stone Guest* by Alexander Dargomyzski (1813–1869), inspired by one of Pushkin's plays, and *Prince Igor*, the only opera by Alexander Borodin (1833–1887). Peter Ilyich Tchaikovsky (1840–1893), who mastered every genre of European music (including symphonies, ballets, and chamber music), made fundamental contributions to Russian opera with such great works as *Eugene Onegin* and *Pique Dame*. In the twentieth century, Sergei Prokofiev (1891–1953; portrait, above) fled the Soviet Union and renewed the Russian operatic tradition with such works as *The Fiery Angel* and *The Love for Three Oranges*. Dmitri Shostakovich (1906–1975) composed a comic opera, *The Nose,* and the tragedy *Lady Macbeth of Mtsensk.*

PUCCINI AND *VERISMO*

The international success of Giacomo Puccini around the turn of the twentieth century marked a new era in operatic history. Puccini managed to combine the "spontaneity" of Italian melody with orchestral writing that reflected the latest musical innovations, rich in instrumental colors and harmonic subtleties. He sought out exotic settings for his operas, which won over audiences with their tense plots, building to overwhelming emotional intensity. Puccini's success encouraged other Italian musicians who, inspired by the *verismo* movement, depicted peasant life and created a new style of singing.

NEW YORK
The most important theater in the United States, the Metropolitan Opera, commissioned a new opera from Puccini in 1910.

♦ **HIS LIFE**
Giacomo Puccini (1858–1924) was the last great Italian composer of operas. He was born in Lucca to a musical family and scored his first great success with *Manon Lescaut* (1893), which had its premiere at the Teatro Regio in Turin. Three years later, in the same theater, Arturo Toscanini conducted the world premiere of *La bohème.* Puccini's sense of theater was peerless, and he constantly sought out innovative subjects and settings. After *Tosca* (1900), Puccini depicted Japan in *Madame Butterfly,* and American frontier life in *La fanciulla del West.* More experimental in nature was his *Trittico,* which consists of three contrasting, one-act operas: *Il tabarro, Suor Angelica,* and *Gianni Schicchi.* Puccini did not live to complete his final opera, *Turandot,* set in Peking and inspired by one of Carlo Gozzi's fables.

♦ **TOSCA**
This story of passion and death is set in three different locations in early nineteenth-century Rome.

♦ **PUCCINI**
Puccini chose a very unusual setting for *La fanciulla del West:* California at the time of the gold rush, foreshadowing the epic Western film.

♦ **A LIBRETTIST**
Puccini was extremely demanding and constantly meddled in the work of his most trusted collaborators.

♦ **IMMIGRATION**
In the early twentieth century, the precarious economic conditions in Italy led many Italians to emigrate to the United States.

♦ **ARTURO TOSCANINI** (1867–1957)
The legendary conductor introduced Italy to the music of Wagner, then worked for many years in the United States. He conducted Puccini's new opera at the Metropolitan, and led the world premiere of *Turandot* (left incomplete) at La Scala in 1926.

♦ **ENRICO CARUSO** (1873–1921)
A native of Naples, Caruso was the ideal tenor for Puccini's operas and other *verismo* works. He was the first *divo* of the recording era.

♦ **NEWSPAPERS**
Puccini was an international sensation, and the world's papers followed his every move.

♦ *CAVALLERIA RUSTICANA*
This opera by Pietro Mascagni (1863–1945), set in rural Sicily, is the masterpiece of *verismo* opera.

EARLY TWENTIETH-CENTURY PARIS

No artistic career could be considered complete without a major Parisian success. At the turn of the century, no city offered a greater variety of performances than the French capital. Revivals of the standard operatic repertory went hand in hand with new works influenced by the latest artistic and literary trends; the acclaimed impressionist school of painting and symbolist poetry, for example, had a profound influence on composer Claude Debussy. In their quest for novel forms and expressive freedom, the new generation of composers paid close attention to innovative works in all the arts, including painting and dance.

◆ **FRENCH OPERA**
The masterpiece of French opera in the nineteenth century is *Carmen* by Georges Bizet (1838–1875), an *opéra-comique* (that is, an opera with spoken dialogue) with a libretto by Henri Meilhac and Ludovic Halévy, drawn from a story by Prosper Merimée, set in Spain among toreadors and cigarette girls. Another important composer is Charles Gounod (1818–1893), who wrote *Faust*, inspired by Goethe, and *Roméo et Juliette*, inspired by Shakespeare. Along with *opéra-comique*, operetta was a popular form in France, as exemplified by the rich productions of Jacques Offenbach (1819–1880), author of *Orphée aux Enfers, La belle Hélène, La vie parisienne*, and an *opéra-comique, Les contes d'Hoffmann* (*The Tales of Hoffmann*). Above, a watercolor by Merimée from 1846, showing a scene from *Carmen*.

PARIS
The French capital was home to a wide variety of theaters that presented the latest and most interesting works. Those out for a stroll could check the posters on the kiosks for news about what was playing.

◆ **MAURICE RAVEL**
(1875–1937)
Ravel wrote two one-act operas: one, *L'enfant et les sortilèges*, featured singing toys and objects from a child's room.

◆ **CLAUDE DEBUSSY**
(1862–1918)
Pelléas et Mélisande, first staged in 1902, represented an alternative to the model of Wagnerian opera.

◆ **MAURICE MAETERLINCK**
(1862–1949)
Debussy was profoundly fascinated by the work of this Belgian author, whose *Pelléas et Mélisande* inspired his only completed opera.

♦ **THE FIREBIRD**
Stravinsky's first composition for the Ballets Russes scored an enormous success in 1910.

♦ **CARMEN**
First performed in 1875, *Carmen* soon became the most popular opera in the French repertory.

♦ **LA VIE PARISIENNE**
From 1866, this operetta by Jacques Offenbach poked fun at the customs and vices of Parisian society.

♦ **PELLÉAS ET MÉLISANDE**
His desire to faithfully reproduce the text of Maeterlinck's drama led Debussy to create a new style of declamation for the characters in *Pelléas et Mélisande.*

♦ **THE BALLETS RUSSES**
The company founded by Serge Diaghilev (1872–1929), an innovative impresario and artistic director, marked a new era in the history of the theater in the early twentieth century. Active on the Parisian scene starting in 1909, the Ballets Russes featured such dancers as Vaslav Nijinsky (1889–1950), and such composers as Igor Stravinsky (1882–1971) and Debussy himself. Set designs were created by avant garde painters like Pablo Picasso and Henri Matisse, who followed in the innovative ways of the impressionists and Cézanne. The Ballets Russes put forth a "symphonic" conception of choreography, intimately tied to music; the strong relationship between dance and music they espoused would eventually lead to many composers losing interest in opera. Above, a 1911 design by Léon Bakst for *Narcisse.*

THE TWENTIETH CENTURY

Musicians explored new horizons in the twentieth century, thanks in part to the innovations in harmony put forth by Arnold Schoenberg, who created a new theory of music based on the exploration of every possible combination of tones. Opera, for the most part, lost its status as popular entertainment and became an increasingly arcane, inaccessible art form. Still, composers like Richard Strauss, though aware of the latest musical developments, followed a somewhat different path and managed to write operas as successful as those of old.

♦ **THE AVANT GARDE**
In the early twentieth century, Arnold Schoenberg (1874–1951; portrait, above) elaborated the dodecaphonic (or twelve-tone) system of composition, based on the "emancipation of dissonance." Expressive possibilities were expanded with *sprechgesang,* "spoken song," employed by Schoenberg in *Pierrot lunaire* and in his unfinished opera, *Moses und Aron.* Alban Berg (1885–1935) explored the innovative possilities of the twelve-tone system in his masterpieces *Wozzeck,* inspired by the drama by Georg Büchner, and the grimly sensual *Lulu.* Igor Stravinsky's *The Rake's Progress,* with its set pieces in the style of the eighteenth century, represented a reaction to these developments, and reexamined the myths of Faust and Don Giovanni. In the end, this eclectic Russian composer eventually adopted Schoenberg's twelve-tone system.

♦ **THEODOR W. ADORNO**
(1903–1969)
A philosopher, Adorno studied music with Schoenberg and became the most radical theoretician of the new style.

♦ **SCHOENBERG**
Active in Vienna, Berlin, and Paris, from 1934 on,

Schoenberg lived in exile in the United States, where he taught at UCLA.

A TENNIS MATCH
On opposite sides of the net, Arnold Schoenberg, master of the twelve-tone system, and George Gershwin, king of the musical. Gershwin envied Schoenberg's method of composition, while Schoenberg craved Gershwin's commercial success. They met in Beverly Hills in the 1930s, where many artists and thinkers had taken refuge from the Nazi regime.

♦ **THOMAS MANN**
(1872–1955)
The German author wrote *Doktor Faust,* inspired by Schoenberg's and Adorno's ideas, in 1947.

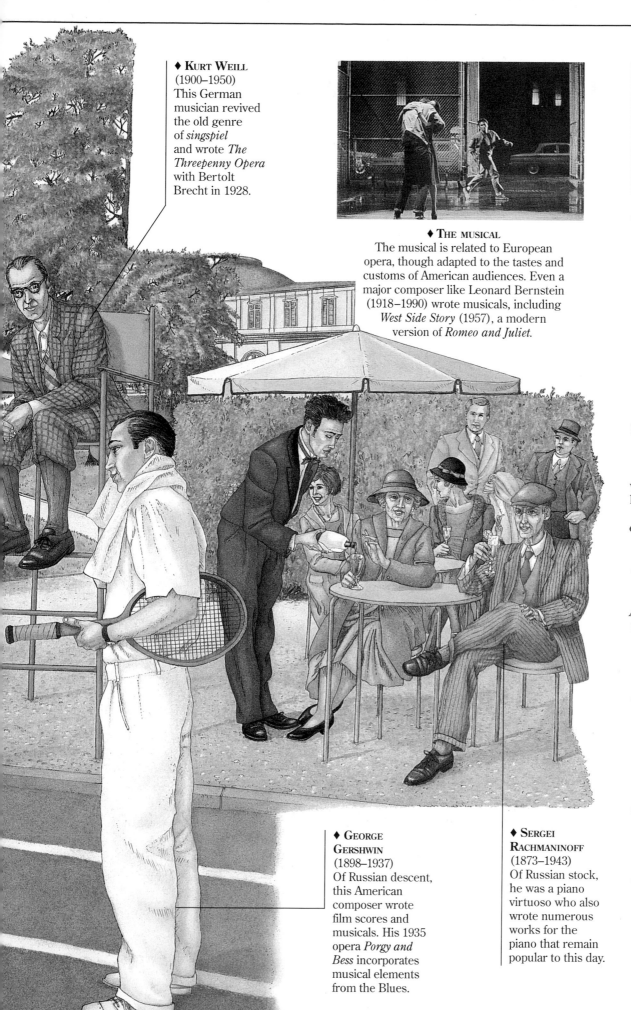

♦ **Kurt Weill**
(1900–1950)
This German musician revived the old genre of *singspiel* and wrote *The Threepenny Opera* with Bertolt Brecht in 1928.

♦ **The musical**
The musical is related to European opera, though adapted to the tastes and customs of American audiences. Even a major composer like Leonard Bernstein (1918–1990) wrote musicals, including *West Side Story* (1957), a modern version of *Romeo and Juliet.*

♦ **Richard Strauss**
(1864–1949)
He was a celebrated conductor and composer of tone poems before turning his hand to opera. For *Salomé* (1905), based on Oscar Wilde's play, with a text by Hugo von Hofmannsthal, he created a quasi-expressionistic musical language. His collaboration with Hofmannsthal led him to a nostalgic exploration of eighteenth-century Vienna in *Der Rosenkavalier,* an elaborate comedy touched with melancholy. In *Ariadne auf Naxos,* the composer and his librettist brought together characters from *opera buffa* and *opera seria,* while *Die Frau ohne Schatten* is a fantastic, highly symbolic tale. In *Capriccio,* a "conversation in music," the elderly composer revisited the eternal operatic problem: which takes priority in opera, the words or the music?

♦ **George Gershwin**
(1898–1937)
Of Russian descent, this American composer wrote film scores and musicals. His 1935 opera *Porgy and Bess* incorporates musical elements from the Blues.

♦ **Sergei Rachmaninoff**
(1873–1943)
Of Russian stock, he was a piano virtuoso who also wrote numerous works for the piano that remain popular to this day.

HOW AN OPERA IS BORN

In the past, new works by contemporary composers were the major attractions in every opera season. Today, new and original stagings of classic operas represent the mainstay of the repertory. A new production of an opera is the result of a long and complex process involving singers, musicians, and technicians. In the earliest stages, the stage director, set designer, and costume designer present their proposal to the theater's management, who then choose the principal artists for the new production. Specialized craftspeople subsequently create the scenery and costumes. Finally, the singers, orchestra musicians, and chorus start the rehearsals that will bring together the different elements of the musical and theatrical event conceived by the director and conductor.

THE THEATER
The staging of an opera at a major theater like La Scala is the result of a complicated undertaking involving hundreds of people and extremely large sums of money. The preparations take place in different stages, each of which involves different departments of the theater. Two years or more can pass from initial concept to premiere.

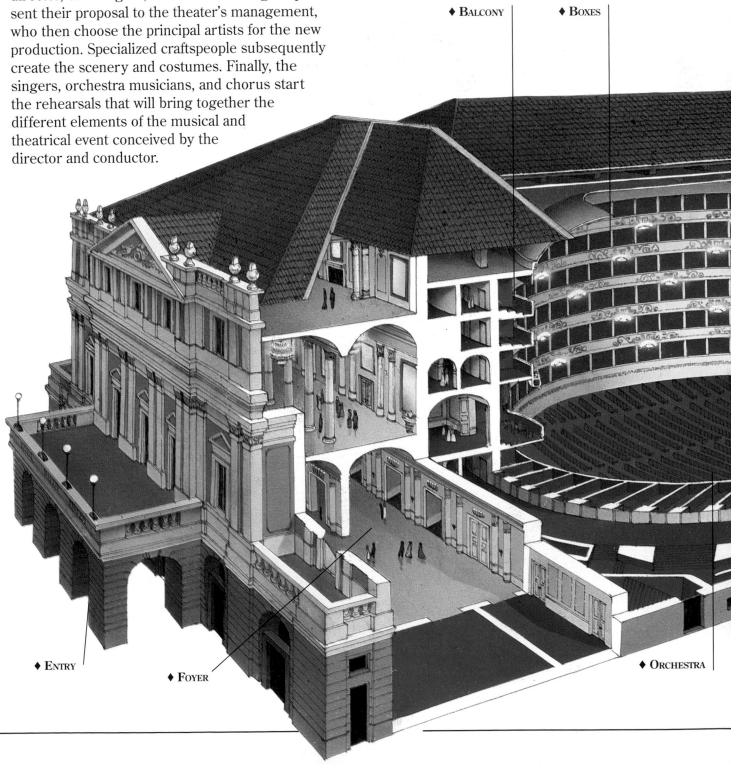

♦ BALCONY   ♦ BOXES

♦ ENTRY

♦ FOYER

♦ ORCHESTRA

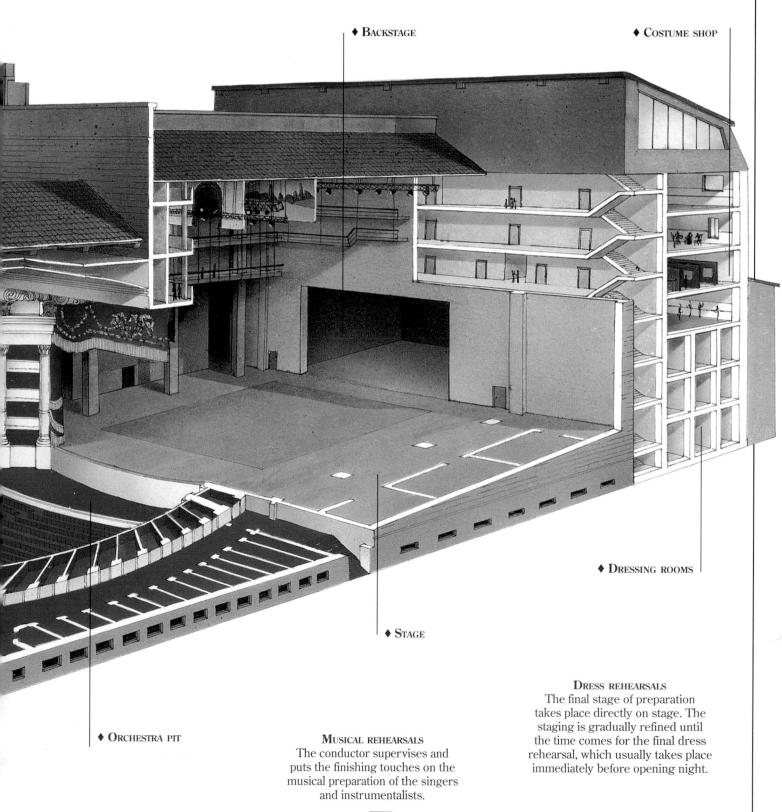

THE CONCEPT
The theater management chooses the cast, which includes the singers, the conductor, and the stage director. The director, along with the set and costume designers, presents a proposal for the new production.

THE PRODUCTION
After the proposal is made, management determines the time and resources needed for the construction of sets and costumes. A schedule for stage and musical rehearsals is established.

STAGE REHEARSALS
The director explains his or her interpretation of the work, and guides the singers through stage rehearsals.

♦ **BACKSTAGE**

♦ **COSTUME SHOP**

♦ **DRESSING ROOMS**

♦ **STAGE**

♦ **ORCHESTRA PIT**

MUSICAL REHEARSALS
The conductor supervises and puts the finishing touches on the musical preparation of the singers and instrumentalists.

DRESS REHEARSALS
The final stage of preparation takes place directly on stage. The staging is gradually refined until the time comes for the final dress rehearsal, which usually takes place immediately before opening night.

SCENERY

The scenery creates the environment in which the drama is set, so the set designer works closely with the director and the costume designer. In the past, set designs consisted of perspective drawings painted directly onto huge canvases. Modern tastes generally require the use of three-dimensional sets, which create a more realistic effect. The work of set designers has always been strongly conditioned by exchanges and contacts with visual artists; today, many set designers take full advantage of recent innovations in lighting and digital technologies.

THE WORKSHOP
Special rooms within the opera house and off-site are used for the creation of scenery. In this case, the opera being staged is Verdi's *Aida*.

◆ THE MODEL
The scale model of the scenery as it will appear onstage serves as a reference for those in the workshop.

◆ THE SET DESIGNER
The set designer is usually chosen by the director, and frequently has a background in architecture and the visual arts.

◆ THE DIRECTOR
The set design can be a critically important part of the director's concept for a given opera.

♦ **DE CHIRICO**
Many great painters have made important contributions to the art of set design. Above, a sketch by Giorgio De Chirico for Bellini's *I puritani*.

♦ **HEAD OF THE SCENERY SHOP**
This professional is responsible for the physical realization of all the scenery.

♦ **BACKDROPS**
Their color can vary depending on the lights used at different times in the performance.

♦ **PAINTERS**
The painters carry out the instructions of the set designer for the colors and designs of the backdrops and other elements.

♦ **A SET DESIGN**
The Austrian painter Oscar Kokoska (1886–1980) created this set design for Verdi's *Un ballo in maschera*.

♦ **HISTORY**
Set design, like opera, was born in Florence, with elborate stage machinery invented at the end of the sixteenth century by Bernardo Buontalenti for performances at the Uffizi. In the early seventeenth century, another Italian, Giacomo Torelli, created the illusion of perspective (with a central vanishing point) onstage. Thanks to the work of the Bibiena family in the eighteenth century, set design and the construction of theaters were fused into a single art. In the twentieth century, the introduction of electric lighting and of elements that can be lifted above stage level paved the way for the innovations of Adolphe Appia. The history of set design includes the names of such illustrious artists as Pablo Picasso, Giorgio De Chirico, and David Hockney. In recent years, the influence of the avant garde has been strong: Robert Wilson (United States), David Borovski (Russia), Josef Svoboda (Poland), and Gae Aulenti (Italy). Above, a sketch by Buontalenti.

COSTUMES

Like scenery, costume designs serve to define the general atmosphere of an operatic production, its placement in time, and the personalities of the characters. In the past, singers owned their own costumes, which were generic enough to be adapted to many different contexts. Today's operatic world demands that each element of a performance be precisely defined and an integral part of the overall production concept. Hence, the need for the costume designer to work closely with the director who, together with the set designer, usually reserves the right to choose costumes for individual characters from among a series of sketches and figures. Many of today's productions feature the work of renowned fashion designers, whose names can also be a "draw" for the public.

♦ **A** COSTUME
This costume was designed by sculptor Giacomo Manzù for Wagner's *Tristan und Isolde*, and created in the celebrated workshop of Umberto Tirelli, who works with today's finest costume designers.

♦ **THE COSTUME DESIGNER**
He or she must take lighting into account when choosing fabrics. Singers often wear several different costumes in the course of an opera.

♦ **THE DRESSMAKER**
Those who make costumes often use a sketch or a figurine as their model. Theatrical costumes are generally much more detailed than normal clothes.

♦ **ACCESSORIES**
Jewelry and other accessories are used to decorate costumes, and provide the final touch for creating a convincing character onstage.

♦ **A** SKETCH
This costume
design for Princess
Turandot was
created by
Umberto
Brunelleschi
for the Maggio
Musicale
Fiorentino
in 1940.

AT THE THEATER
In dressing rooms and in the make-up
room, soloists and members of the
chorus prepare to take the stage.
The preparation of the new staging
of *Aïda* is now in its final stages.

♦ **WIGS**
Wigs complete
the artist's make-
up and help define
the personality
and social position
of a character.

♦ **THE** MAKE-UP
ARTIST
Well before each
performance, he
or she makes up
the artists who
will be appearing
onstage.

THE FINAL DRESS REHEARSAL

In the operatic world, as in the theatrical world in general, the stage director is a relatively recent figure, who appeared in the early decades of the twentieth century as stagings became more complex, and the need emerged for a person who could coordinate the different elements of a performance. Initially a kind of stage manager, in recent decades the stage director has taken on a distinctly creative role. Each new production represents an original interpretation of a given opera, and the director's task is to create the overall concept through the individual elements of scenery, costumes, and performance style. Production schedules and costs, though, can often limit what the director wishes to achieve.

♦ **TWO DIRECTORS**
The German artist Max Reinhardt (1873–1943) worked extensively in legitimate theater and helped to define the role of the modern director. Luca Ronconi (1933–) is one of the most unconventional and fascinating directors on the contemporary European theatrical scene.

REHEARSALS
The conductor and director lead rehearsals, which begin weeks before the premiere and involve soloists, the chorus, and the orchestra.

♦ **THE PROSCENIUM**
The proscenium is the area of the stage closest to the audience.

♦ **THE DIRECTOR AND ASSISTANT DIRECTOR**
The assistant director takes notes on the director's instructions, which can be consulted at any time.

♦ **REFLECTORS**
In today's theaters, lighting is controlled via computer.

♦ **LUCHINO VISCONTI**
(1906–1976) Visconti was among the first to bring the realism of legitimate theater to the operatic stage, and to enhance the dignity of the overall performance. His love for music emerged in a number of his films, including *Senso* (1954), and he revealed his great gifts as an opera director in a series of productions built around soprano Maria Callas (1923–1977), most notably Verdi's *La traviata* (1955), Bellini's *La sonnambula*, and Donizetti's *Anna Bolena*, all for La Scala, as well as several other nineteenth-century Italian operas. Many directors are indebted to his stagings, including Franco Zeffirelli, his former assistant, who directed two operatic films based on Verdi (*La traviata* and *Otello*), following in the footsteps of Joseph Losey, who brought *Don Giovanni* to the silver screen.

♦ **THE CHORUS**
Rehearsing a scene together from *Aida* by Giuseppe Verdi.

♦ **THE PROMPTER'S BOX**
Located beneath the stage, it hides the prompter, who "feeds" lines to the singers as needed.

OPERA TODAY

The demise of traditional musical languages has brought about a radical change in the meaning and function of opera. Some composers maintain that opera should be set aside once and for all, as an irrelevant relic of the past. But others continue to struggle with the expressive possibilities inherent in opera, and in doing so manage to revitalize this traditional art form. Opera, born four centuries ago as the union of words and music, is an increasingly problematic art, but it endures in new and stimulating guises.

THE "TRAGEDY OF LISTENING" This was the definition given by the creators of *Prometeo*, by Venetian composer Luigi Nono (1925–1990). Sounds arrive from all directions in a listening space that has been totally redefined, one in which the public does not "attend" a musical event but is actually caught up in it.

♦ **MUSICIANS** During *Prometeo*, musicians are positioned all around the audience and move about throughout the performance, creating new sources of sound.

♦ **THE MUSICAL ARK** This enormous sound box was designed by architect Renzo Piano. It allows for the definition of a specific acoustical space within a larger structure, such as a church or an industrial facility.

♦ **THE PUBLIC** Spectators sit in the middle of the space and are surrounded by music.

◆ **ELECTRONIC DEVICES**
They are operated in real time to break up the sound into its component parts and to create constant (but almost imperceptible) variations.

THE CHURCH
The first performance of *Prometeo* took place in 1984 in Venice's church of San Lorenzo. The second performance took place the following year in Milan, in a hangar at Ansaldo.

◆ **THE STRUCTURE**
Built of wood, it created a huge ark within the church.

◆ **NEW HORIZONS**
The post-war operatic world offers a richly varied panorama. The introduction of electronic instruments has brought new dimensions to musical thought: German composer Karl Heinz Stockausen (1928–) made heavy use of electronic elements in his colossal opera, *Licht*, divided into seven days and unfinished as of this writing. The approach of Hans Werner Henze (1926–) is more traditional, relying as it does on plays by Kleist and on ancient theater. The American Philip Glass (1937– , above) collaborated with avant garde director Robert Wilson (1941–) on *Einstein on the Beach*, a revolutionary work. *La vera storia* and *Un re in ascolto* by Italian composer Luciano Berio (1925–) make use of unconventional forms of theater.

A BRIEF HISTORY OF OPERA

THE BIRTH OF *MELODRAMMA*

An original fusion of music, song, and staged action led to the creation of opera or *melodramma,* whose birthplace is generally considered to be Florence, among the groups of artists and aristocrats who sought to recreate ancient tragedy. The dream became reality with the dominance of monodic or single-voiced song, as opposed to the polyphonic (or many-voiced) music then in vogue, which was not suitable for dramatic performances. Though there were earlier experiments in the genre, the first opera to come down to us in its entirety is *Euridice* by Ottavio Rinuccini (1563–1621), with music by Jacopo Peri (1561–1633), which was performed at the Pitti Palace in 1600 during the marriage festivities of Maria de' Medici and Henri IV of France [➤ 6/7]. This was the first in a series of performances that helped to establish the new style of *recitar cantando* ("acting while singing") [➤ 6/7]. The first masterpiece in the newborn genre was *Orfeo,* a *favola in musica* by Alessandro Striggio and Claudio Monteverdi (1567–1643) [➤ 8], presented at the Gonzaga court in Mantova. In the same year, Monteverdi wrote the opera *Arianna,* in which Virginia Ramponi Andreini (1583–1628) created the title role. In the early years of opera, composers themselves were often performers: Jacopo Peri was a much-admired tenor; and Giulio Caccini (1550–1618), who also wrote an opera called *Euridice,* was a singer and played the viol.

THE SEVENTEENTH CENTURY

Monteverdi was the first great protagonist of the next stage in operatic history, which took place after the first public theater opened in Venice, in 1637 [➤ 8/9]. The San Cassiano theater offered performances to anyone who paid for a ticket, not just to courtiers. Opera began to leave behind the pastoral settings of its earliest years, absorbing popular elements and intermingling tragic and comic scenes. Among

the fruits of Venetian opera were Monteverdi's two masterpieces, *Il ritorno di Ulisse in patria* and *L'incoronazione di Poppea* (1643), along with many works by Monteverdi's pupils, who included Francesco Cavalli (1602–1676), composer of 39 operas (of which 26 have come down to us in manuscript form). Serious arias and comic *canzonette* alternate in *Egisto* (1643), *Ormindo* (1644), *Giasone* (1649), *Xerse* (1655), and *Ercole amante* (1662). Among the works of Giovanni Legrenzi (1626–1690), *La divisione del mondo* (1675) and *Germanico sul Reno* (1676) have come down to us, while Antonio Cesti (1623–1669) composed *Orontea* (1656) and *Il pomo d'oro* (1668). Sumptuous stagings and a gradual increase in the number of arias are some of the characteristics of Venetian opera at this time, and these fashions soon spread to Rome and all over Europe. In France, Jean-Baptiste Lully (1632–1687) established the fundamentals of *tragédie en musique,* which consisted of allegorical scenes and dances and faithfully reflected the absolutist spirit of Louis XIV's reign [➤ 10/11]. Lully's greatest works include *Atys* (1676), *Bellerophon* (1679), *Proserpine* (1680), *Armide* (1686), and are inspired by mythological, historical, and chivalric tales. Jean-Philippe Rameau (1683–1764) renewed the tradition with *Les Indes galantes* (1735), *Zoroastre* (1749), *Castor et Pollux* (1737) [➤ 21]. In England, Italian opera took second place to the masque, which (like the French *tragédie en musique,* though with greater freedom) alternated song, dance, and pantomime. Henry Purcell (1659–1695) was its greatest exponent [➤ 11].

ITALIAN PRIMACY

In eighteenth-century Europe, which was politically fragmented, Italian opera retained its primacy. The librettists responsible for the *opera seria* canon were Italian: Apostolo Zeno (1668–1750) and Pietro Metastasio (1698–1782); they gave a more regular form to its action and to the characters'

Jean-Philippe Rameau, heir to the tradition established by Lully, in an eighteenth-century portrait.

Ludwig Schnorr and his wife Malvina in Wagner's *Tristan.*

The Teatro La Fenice of Venice, before its destruction in a fire on January 29, 1996.

An illustration from the first edition of Gluck's *Orfeo ed Euridice,* published in Paris in 1764.

speeches [➤ 16]. Such German composers as Georg Friedrich Händel (1685–1759) [➤ 14], Johann Adolph Hasse (1699–1783), and Mozart himself (1756–1791) [➤ 22] also composed Italian operas; Mozart's greatest masterworks are written in the Italian language.

In this phase of operatic history, arias increased in number and in length, and were characterized by highly florid singing. They covered the full range of passions of operatic characters, but soon became a pretext for mere vocal exhibition, and began to dominate at the expense of recitatives. Among the operas by Alessandro Scarlatti (1660–1725) [➤ 17]: *Gli equivoci nel sembiante* (1679), *Mitridate Eupatore* (1707), *Tigrane* (1715), *Il trionfo dell'onore* (1718), and *Griselda* (1721). *Semiramide riconosciuta* (1729) and *Ariadne in Naxus* (1733) are the masterworks of Nicola Porpora (1686–1768). Among the forty-five dramatic works by Georg Friedrich Händel [➤ 14]: *Rinaldo* (1711), *Giulio Cesare in Egitto* (1724), *Rodelinda regina de' longobardi* (1725), *Alcina* (1735), *Serse* (1738), and *Deidamia* (1741). Johann Adolph Hasse, a friend of librettist Pietro Metastasio, was no less important a composer at the time; he left such works as *Antioco* (1721), *Artaserse* (1730), *Arminio* (1730), *La clemenza di Tito* (1735), and *Ruggiero* (1771). *Opera buffa* was also Italian, and enjoyed international success thanks to the *intermezzi* of *La serva padrona* (1733) by Giovan Battista Pergolesi (1710–1736) [➤ 17], the Neapolitan composer who was to serve as a model for the generation that included Giovanni Paisiello (1740–1816) and Domenico Cimarosa (1749–1801), who wrote *Il matrimonio segreto* (1792) [➤ 18/19].

FROM GLUCK'S "REFORM" TO MOZART'S GENIUS
In the seventeenth and eighteenth centuries *castrati* were in great vogue, renowned for their extraordinary vocal gifts and adored by audiences. Among the most famous castrati were Farinelli (1705–1782), Senesino (c. 1680– c. 1750), and Caffarelli (1710–1783) [➤ 14/15]. The eighteenth-century stage was also dominated by authentic prima donnas, who emphasized vocal virtuosity at the expense of expressiveness: Francesca Cuzzoni (1700–1770), Faustina Bordoni (1700–1781), Vittoria Tesi (1700–1775), and Lucrezia Aguiari (1743–1783), who was admired by Mozart. Christoph Willibald Gluck (1714–1787) [➤ 20/21] sought to check the dominance of singers and to renew the time-worn traditions of operatic theater through a more declamatory style of singing and greater attention to orchestration (*Orfeo ed Euridice*, 1762; *Alceste,* 1767). Gluck established the foundations for a true musical "reform," which provoked great interest and debate among Enlightenment figures. Wolfgang Amadeus Mozart (1756–1791) began his rich operatic output by taking on all the different genres, from *opera seria* (*Idomeneo,* 1781, and *La clemenza di Tito,* 1791) to *opera buffa* (*The Marriage of Figaro,* 1786); in *Don Giovanni* (1787), he created a unique fusion of the two styles [➤ 22]. *Così fan tutte* (1790) completed the trilogy of works created in collaboration with Lorenzo Da Ponte (1749–1838) [➤ 30/31]. Mozart also set the course for the future development of German national opera with *Die Entführung aus dem Serail* (1782), a *singspiel,* or German-language theatrical genre in which spoken dialogue alternates with musical selections and where fantastic and popular elements intermingle. *The Magic Flute* (1791), another *singspiel,* is a multi-layered fable and the composer's theatrical testament. The English ballad opera (derived from the masque), the Spanish *zarzuela,* and the French *opéra-comique* had similar struc-

Moscow's Bolshoi Theater in the early twentieth century.

tures. In Mozart's time, in the second half of the eighteenth-century, several of the most important opera houses of all time were built, to accommodate the ever-larger audiences. The traditional architectural scheme is that of the Italian-style hall, with several different levels of boxes surrounding the orchestra in the form of a horseshoe. In Milan, the Teatro alla Scala [➤ 48/49] opened in 1778, boasting 146 boxes and a long tradition of premieres of works by Bellini, Donizetti, Verdi, Puccini, and others. The Teatro Comunale of Bologna (1763) was constructed of stone (and not the traditional gilded plaster) by Antonio Galli Bibiena (1700–1774). A recent fire destroyed the Teatro La Fenice in Venice, which opened in 1792. In Munich, the Cuvillés Theatre, which dates from 1753, is a splendid rococo-style hall; Berlin's Staatsoper Unter den Linden, built in 1742 and restored in 1844, offers an interior in the sober, elegant Neoclassical manner.

Verdi and nineteenth-century Italian opera

The dominance of Italian opera continued into the nineteenth century, first with Gioacchino Rossini (1792–1868), who turned the principles that had underpinned the birth of opera on their head, giving free play to his melodic fancy, sustained by a refined orchestral accompaniment [➤ 24/25]. Rossini's career was something of a triumphal march, from his first Venetian *farse* to *Tancredi* (1813), and from *L'italiana in Algeri* (1813) and *Il barbiere di Siviglia* (1816) to the *opere serie* he wrote for Naples, including *Ermione* (1819) and *La donna del lago* (1819). The "march," though, came to a premature end in Paris, where Rossini abandoned his operatic career after his local debut, *William Tell* (1829). His favorite artist, Isabella Colbran (1785–1845) became one of opera's very first "divas." Her contemporary, Giuditta Pasta (1797–1845), created many roles for composer Vincenzo Bellini (1801–1835) [➤ 27]. Bellini, too, died in Paris after a brief but intense life that saw him imbue numerous operas with Romantic passion (*Il pirata*, 1827; *La sonnambula*, 1831; *Norma*, 1831) and temper the vivaciousness of Rossini's *bel canto* style. The career of Gaetano Donizetti (1797–1848) followed a similar course: he left behind his masterwork, *Lucia di Lammermoor* (1835) among seventy other operas, composed in less than thirty years for Europe's

greatest theaters [➤ 28]. With Giuseppe Verdi (1813–1901), the old image of the operatic composer vanished, replaced by the new figure of the dramatist who supervised the crafting of his librettos with care, creating concise *melodrammi* of great dramatic impact [➤ 34/35]. His *Nabucco* (1842) led the way, as interpreted by soprano Giuseppina Strepponi (1815–1897), Verdi's future wife. The composer continued his musical and dramatic explorations with *Ernani* (1844) and *Macbeth* (1847), and with the more successful *Rigoletto* (1851), *Il trovatore* (1853), and *La traviata* (1853), where the composer showed great originality in setting the most unusual and "scandalous" subjects. *Un ballo in maschera* (1859), *Don Carlos* (1867), *Aida* (1871), *Otello* (1887), and *Falstaff* (1893) represented further stages in the theatrical career of Verdi, much loved in Italy also for the evocations of the *Risorgimento* (Italian independence movement) in some of his works.

France

Paris is the capital of *grand-opéra,* a theatrical genre that was perfected by Giacomo Meyerbeer (1791–1864) who chose, along with librettist Eugène Scribe (1791–1861), spectacular subjects with historical backgrounds, and made of them true "colossals" [➤ 32/33]. Adolphe Nourrit (1802–1839) was the most famous tenor to perform in this typically French genre. Very soon, though, he was supplanted in public favor by Gilbert-Louis Duprez (1806–1896) [➤ 32/33]. Most composers of the nineteenth century, including Wagner and Verdi, tried their hand at *grand-opéra,* while Hector Berlioz (1803–1869) [➤ 33], an ingenious orchestrator and symphonic composer, offered his personal vision of the lyric theater with the epic *Les Troyens* (1890). The masterpieces of French opera in the second half of the nineteenth century are *Faust* (1859) by Charles Gounod (1818–1893), and *Carmen* by Georges Bizet (1838–1875) [➤ 44], with the latter representing the culmination of the *opéra-comique* genre. The rich productions of Jules Massenet (1842–1912), author of *Werther* (1892), falls somewhere between intimism and decadence.

New York's (old) Metropolitan Opera in 1889.

The diva Maria Callas (1923–1977)

Tenor Luciano Pavarotti (1935–)

WAGNER AND GERMAN OPERA

In Germany, a national school of opera sprang up, whose greatest representative was Carl Maria von Weber (1786–1826), who created a Romantic style of musical theater that included elements from folktales [➤ 29]. His masterpieces are *Der Freischütz* (1821), *Oberon* (1826), and *Euryanthe* (1823). Even before Weber, one must not overlook the contribution of Ludwig van Beethoven (1770–1827) [➤ 28/29] and his sole opera, *Fidelio* (1805). Such composers paved the way for Richard Wagner (1813–1883) [➤ 36/37], who surpassed all previous "reformers" of opera in asserting and defending the concept of absolutely unified drama, the goal of his major works from *Der Ring des Niebelungen* (1848–1874) to *Tristan und Isolde* (1865) and *Parsifal* (1882). *Parsifal* was the first opera conceived for the theater that Wagner had built on the hill of Bayreuth, a small German town, where the composer sought to renew the spirit of ancient rite and where the public, without class distinctions, would take its place in a hall with an invisible orchestra. Among the interpreters most admired by Wagner himself: Wilhelmine Schröder-Devrient (1804–1860), tenor Ludwig Schnorr von Carolsfeld (1835–1865) and his wife Malvina (1825–1904). During the years when Wagner achieved his dream of a new type of theater—the Festspielhaus, opened in 1876—all over Europe more traditional theaters were being built: London's Covent Garden, which opened in 1858 on the site of three earlier theaters (all destroyed), dating back to 1732; Moscow's Bolshoi Theater, from 1856; Saint Petersburg's Marinski Theater, from 1860; and the Opéra-Garnier in Paris, from 1875.

RUSSIA

The history of Russian opera begins in the eighteenth century, when the major Italian composers made visits to Russian theaters. But with Mikhail Glinka (1804–1857) and his *A Life for the Czar* (1836), the Russian national school of opera was born. Throughout the nineteenth century, Russian composers, including Modest Mussorgsky (1839–1881), Alexander Borodin (1833–1887), and Peter Ilyich Tchaikovsky (1840–1893), would draw on Russian history, folklore, and literature [➤ 40/41]. The works of Alexander Pushkin (1799–1837) inspired *Boris Godunov* (1874) by Mussorgsky, and Tchaikovsky's *Eugene Onegin* (1879) and *Queen of Spades* (1890). In the twentieth century, Dmitri Shostakovich (1906–1975) based *The Nose* (1930) on a story by Nikolai Gogol (1801–1852) and also composed the dramatic *Lady Macbeth of Mtsensk* (1934), while Sergei Prokofiev (1891–1953) wrote *The Fiery Angel* (1955) and the grand historical fresco *War and Peace* (1946), based on the novel of the same name by the great Russian writer Leo Tolstoy (1882–1945).

THE TWENTIETH CENTURY

The dawn of the new century once again saw the dominance of an Italian composer: Giacomo Puccini (1858–1924) [➤ 42/43], who gave opera its last popular successes with *La bohème* (1896), *Tosca* (1900), *Madame Butterfly* (1904), and *Turandot* (1920), works that combine expert orchestration with an inspired melodic vein. The exceptional voice of Enrico Caruso (1873–1921) contributed to the success of Puccini's operas; one of Caruso's heirs was Beniamino Gigli (1890–1957). Along with Puccini's works, there was the *verismo* school, which started with *Cavalleria rusticana* (1890) by Pietro Mascagni (1863–1945). In France, Claude Debussy (1862–1918) [➤ 44/45] created *Pelléas et Mélisande* (1902), while in Germany Richard

The conductors Claudio Abbado (1933–; left) and Herbert von Karajan (1908–1989).

Strauss (1864–1949) [→ 47] was heir to the Wagnerian tradition, which he surpassed with the expressionistic, decadent worlds of *Salome* (1905) and *Elektra* (1909). With *Der Rosenkavalier* (1911) Strauss's works changed radically, undertaking a nostalgic "dialogue" with works of the operatic past. After the First World War, it was great singers above all who kept operatic tradition alive. Among the stars of the 1950s, 1960s, and 1970s, some of whom are active today: sopranos Elisabeth Schwarzkopf (1915–), Renata Tebaldi (1922–), Birgit Nilsson (1918–), Régine Crespin (1927–), Mirella Freni (1935–), Renata Scotto (1934–), Jessye Norman (1945–), and Joan Sutherland (1926–); mezzo sopranos and contraltos Giulietta Simionato (1910–), Christa Ludwig (1924–), Teresa Berganza (1934–), and Marilyn Horne (1934–); tenors Carlo Bergonzi (1924–), Wolfgang Windgassen (1914–1974), Placido Domingo (1941–), and Luciano Pavarotti (1935–); baritone Dietrich Fischer Dieskau (1925–); and basses Ruggero Raimondi (1941–) and José van Dam (1940–). Among opera's newest stars: mezzo soprano Cecilia Bartoli (1966–) and tenor José Cura (1962–). Maria Callas (1923–1977), who embodied the very essence of a *bel canto* diva, is in a class of her own among artists of the postwar era. Vienna, one of the capitals of the operatic tradition, can be said to have taken up arms against classic melodramma: Arnold Schoenberg (1874–1951) "emancipated" dissonance with the twelve-tone system, and rejected the facile route to communication with the public [→ 46]. Musical theater subsequently became more problematical, reflecting the anxieties, tensions, and rifts of contemporary art. It was an age of "unique" masterpieces: *Wozzeck* (1925) and *Lulu* (1937) by Alban Berg (1885–1935), *Moses und Aron* (1931) by Schoenberg, *Bluebeard's Castle* (1918) by Béla Bartók (1881–1945), and *Cardillac* (1926) by Paul Hindemith (1895–1963). The works of Czech composer Leoš Janáček (1854–1928) are very much *sui generis:* in the early decades of the century, he capitalized on new expressive possibilities in such works as *Jenůfa* (1904), *Kátya Kabanová* (1921), *The Makropoulos Case* (1926), and *From the House of the Dead* (1930). Igor Stravinsky (1882–1971), with *The Rake's Progress* (1951), among the most frequently performed of twentieth-century operas, revisited the "number opera" with clearly parodic intent [→ 46]. Benajmin Britten (1913–1976), after turning to the princi-

ples of ballad opera with his 1948 reworking of *The Beggar's Opera* (1728) by John Gay (1685–1732), created a new type of chamber drama with *The Turn of the Screw* (1954), and enriched the twentieth-century repertory with such works as *Peter Grimes* (1945), *Billy Budd* (1951), and *A Midsummer Night's Dream* (1960). In terms of new operatic theaters, 1908 saw the construction of the largest opera house in the world, the Teatro Colon in Buenos Aires, which can hold 3,500 spectators. The new Metropolitan Opera (1966) in New York has a similar capacity; it replaced the old theater, which had opened a century earlier, and where Arturo Toscanini had conducted. The Opéra-Bastille in Paris (1990) is currently considered the most technologically advanced theater, topping the Sydney Opera House (1973).

Notwithstanding great economic investments, organizational efforts, and the construction of new theaters, the twentieth century—with the advent of various avant gardes, the twelve-tone system, and electronic music—has seen contemporary opera lose the popular appeal it inherited from the nineteenth-century tradition. Mass audiences, furthermore, have turned their attention to other forms of theater: to cinema in particular. Musical theater has thus become a kind of battleground for musicians eager to explore the relationship between words and music. New horizons are opening up in many different directions, as shown by the work in recent decades of Karl Heinz Stockhausen (1928–), Hans Werner Henze (1926–), Philip Glass (1937–), Luigi Nono (1925–1990), Györgi Ligeti (1923–), Luciano Berio (1925–), and John Adams (1947–) [→ 56/57].

CONDUCTORS

The conductor in the modern sense of the term was born in the early nineteenth century, in response to the increasing complexity of scores and the growth in size of orchestras. Gasparo Spontini (1784–1851) was the first to lead musicians using a long baton. Hans von Bülow (1830–1894) and Hermann Levi (1839–1900) conducted premieres of operas by Wagner. Gustav Mahler (1860–1911) [→ 39] and Richard Strauss (1864–1949) [→ 47] contributed to the revival of Mozart's operas. Angelo Mariani (1821–1873) was an esteemed interpreter of Verdi's operas. The first conductor to become a real "star" was Arturo Toscanini

(1867–1957) [➤ 43], who presided over the premieres of several Puccini operas. Wilhelm Furtwängler (1886–1954) and Clemens Krauss (1893–1954) belonged to Toscanini's generation, and were unsurpassed as interpreters of the German Romantic repertoire. The Greek composer Dimitri Mitropulos (1896–1960) led memorable performances of Verdi's operas and of twentieth-century works. Herbert von Karajan (1908–1989) offered an intensely lyrical reading of the most important works in the operatic repertoire. The Hungarian Georg Solti (1912–1997) took on an equally vast range of works, while the Italian Carlo Maria Giulini (1914–) focused on a select number of operas. The next generation of illustrious conductors includes the German Carlos Kleiber (1930–), the Italians Claudio Abbado (1933–) and Riccardo Muti (1941–), the American James Levine (1943–), the Argentinian Daniel Barenboim (1942–), the Japanese Seiji Ozawa (1935–), and the Indian Zubin Mehta (1936–).

STAGE DIRECTORS

Though their role has been clearly defined only recently, stage directors today play a fundamental role in the world of opera, because they (along with the conductor) are responsible for presenting to the public a modern, dramatically coherent reading of a given opera. The most illustrious pioneers of the early twentieth century included Edward Gordon Craig (1872–1966) and Max Reinhardt (1873–1943) [➤ 54]; the succeeding generation boasted Luchino Visconti (1906–1976) [➤ 54] in Italy and Wieland Wagner (1917–1966) in Germany. Visconti offered a stimulating and authoritative reading of the Italian operatic tradition, with an emphasis on the works of Verdi—most notably, his celebrated staging of *La traviata* from the 1950s. Wieland Wagner, grandson of the great composer, renewed the image of Wagnerian musical theater in productions dominated by lyrical and abstract elements—truly revolutionary within the performing tradition of the Bayreuth Festival. Giorgio Strehler (1921–1997) was one of the giants among operatic stage directors; his stagings of *Die Entführung aus dem Serail* and *The Marriage of Figaro* achieved the status of classics, and his productions of Verdi's *Simon Boccanegra* and *Macbeth* were equally important. French director Jean-Pierre Ponnelle (1932–1988) was deeply inspired by music, probing the works of Rossini and Wagner with an undeniable theatrical flair, and designing both the sets and the costumes of his operas. More avant garde are the approaches of the German directors Peter Stein (1937–) and Klaus Michael Grüber (1941–), who divide their efforts between operatic and spoken theater, offering an ideologically informed reading of musical works. The Italian Luca Ronconi (1933–) has never lost sight of the theatrical tradition of the Italian baroque, which he has renewed and sometimes turned on its head in his finest productions, including Verdi's *Aida*, Rossini's *Il viaggio a Reims,* and Berlioz's *La damnation de Faust.* French director Patrice Chereau (1944–) shed new light on the interpretation of Wagner's works with his celebrated production of *Der Ring des Niebelungen* for the Bayreuth Festival (1976), whose irreverent spirit provoked scandal and polemics among more conservative

The Japanese conductor Seiji Ozawa (1935–).

Wagnerians. Peter Sellars (1958–) represents the most radical achievements of the American avant garde, and has sought to elucidate the modern character of operatic theater by updating the setting of many works—in the Mozartian trilogy of *The Marriage of Figaro, Don Giovanni,* and *Così fan tutte,* for example, which he set in the modern-day United States.

FESTIVALS

Far fewer operas are written today than a century or two ago. But the drastic drop in production has not lessened interest in the four centuries of operatic repertoire that continues to hold the stage. The programs of opera houses all over the world, ranging from Baroque to twentieth-century works, show no bias against any style or form from the past, and the international operatic festivals confirm this tendency. Among the oldest and most prestigious is the Salzburg Festival, held in Austria since 1917 in the city of Mozart and in his honor, though increasingly open to modern musical styles. In Italy, the Maggio Musicale Fiorentino has focused since its inception on prestigious revivals, while the Arena di Verona's season is aimed at the broader opera-going public. More recent though no less distinguished is the Rossini Opera Festival, held in Pesaro. In England, the Glyndebourne Festival, dating from 1934, maintains its aristocratic grace, while in France, the Aix-en-Provence Festival is famous for its superb revivals of operas by Mozart and French composers. The Bayreuth Festival, founded by Wagner in 1876, the first festival in history devoted to the performance of his own works, is attended by thousands of music lovers every year.

INDEX